381st Bomb

By Ron MacKay
Color By Don Greer
& Tom Tullis

squadron/signal publications

COPYRIGHT 1994 SQUADRON/SIGNAL PUBLICATIONS, INC.
1115 CROWLEY DRIVE CARROLLTON, TEXAS 75011-5010
All rights reserved. No part of this publication may be reproduced, stored in a retrieval system or transmitted in any form by means electrical, mechanical or otherwise, without written permission of the publisher.

ISBN 0-89747--314-0 First Edition

If you have any photographs of aircraft, armor, soldiers or ships of any nation, particularly wartime snapshots, why not share them with us and help make Squadron/Signal's books all the more interesting and complete in the future. Any photograph sent to us will be copied and the original returned. The donor will be fully credited for any photos used. Please send them to:

Squadron/Signal Publications, Inc.
1115 Crowley Drive.
Carrollton, TX 75011-501010

PHOTO CREDITS

National Air and Space Museum	USAF Museum
Dave Morgan	Jack Prillaman
Darrell Debolt	George Porter
Bob Vanbuskirk	Leonard Spivey
Fred Nudell	Cliff Bishop
Steve Gotts	Harry Holmes
Jerry Scutts	Bill Blackmon

DEDICATION

This book is respectfully dedicated to the memory of CAPT Edwin R. Manchester, a 535th BS "original" pilot who was killed in action over Bremen on 8 October 1943. Truly "For my Tomorrow, you gave your Today". My gratitude for a life of freedom also goes to the late General (four star) Joseph J. Nazzaro, Colonel Conway S. Hall (Group COs) and all personnel of the 381st Bomb Group who lived up to their unit motto "Triumphant We Fly" during twenty-two months of unremitting combat.

Overleaf: This formation of four B-17F Flying Fortresses of the 535th BS, was led by CHAPS FLYING CIRCUS which was fatally ditched by LT Carl Baur on 30 Jan 1944. MS:R is TSII in which CAPT Manchester was killed on 8 October 1943, while MS:T was also lost the same day with LT Bill Cormany and MAJ Ingenhutt (Squadron Commander), although both men survived and became POWs.

Introduction

By June 1943 the U.S. 8th Air Force daylight bombing offensive from Britain had passed through a full nine months of "experimentation". In its initial stages, targets had been limited mainly to targets in France and the Low Countries with occasional stabs at points close to or just inside the German borders. A prevailing lack of long-range escort fighters was a factor in restricting operations although the proponents of the "self-defending" bomber formation in which the heavy armament of the B-17 Fortresses and B-24 Liberators would suffice to see them to and from targets with acceptable loss ratios, were still confident of success. Their enthusiasm must have been tempered by the 17 April mission when 16 out of 115 B-17s were Missing in Action (MIA), but only a sustained period of operations under non-escort conditions would settle the issue for better or worse.

April and May of 1943 had seen the arrival in Britain of six more B-17 Groups with three forming the basis of a new 4th wing (soon to be known as the 3rd Bomb Division) and three joining the existing 1st wing. One of the latter trio was the 381st BG. Assignment to the 8th Air Force represented the culmination of very hard training by all ranks of the Group from Colonel to cook, aircraft commander to clerk. Working up in the cold arid plains of Pyote, Texas and then finishing at Pueblo, Colorado, a high standard of aerial and ground efficiency was achieved in which no aircraft were lost and only one fatal casualty was incurred.

The 381st BG was commanded by COL Joseph J. Nazzaro with LCOL Leland Fiegel as Deputy CO and MAJ Conway S. Hall as Group Ops Officer; a trio of men bringing the respective qualities of tactician, pilot ability and combat experience to form a bedrock which was to stand the Group in good stead in combat. This cadre of officers arrived with forward ground echelons in January at Pyote and the first handful of B-17s flew in on the 9th. Ground training initially took priority over flying with personnel having to come to terms with crowded quarters, limited facilities and the weather. Pyote's high winds were so frequent that unshackled buildings were liable to prompt destruction and sand was a constant hazard to living conditions and maintenance of aircraft.

The Fortresses were generally readied for flight between 1200 and 1600 hours when dust storms tended to make their presence felt with 40 mph gusts throwing a screen up to 2,000 feet and then waning as fast as they had waxed. Sending the B-17s aloft had the beneficial effect of allaying the worst sand-blast effects on their sensitive engines. Rain was so rare that local legend told of one Pyote citizen who, when hit by a raindrop, had to be revived by having a bucket of sand thrown over him.

Each morning the ground crew had to herd cattle off the runways, the animals being attracted by the weed patches on the verges, created in turn by water sprayed on the runways to keep dust down. More serious was the malfunctioning of top turret micro switches which caused the guns to continue firing when in direct line with the vertical fin. The resultant damage only added to the workload of the already hard-pressed ground crews and the fliers were probably equally unimpressed. Although radios were available these were of marginal off-duty benefit as the sole station they could pick up during the day churned out what the Northern boys caustically referred to as "Hill-Billy music."

Initial flying training culminated in late January with a total Group effort by five B-17s to help in a sea-search mission out of Muroc, California by which time the four squadrons (532nd to 535th BS) each had five aircraft allocated. Immediately, the Group leaders started a program of training in close formation flying, although it is a matter of conjecture whether COL Nazzaro was aware at this early stage that the 381st BG would be assigned to the 8th Air Force where such tactics were an absolute prerequisite for individual and corporate survival.

At this point in the Second World War, allocation of Bomb Groups to European or Pacific Theaters showed no bias either way; in Europe there were four B-17 and two B-24 Groups with a smaller force in North

The thriving city of Pyote, Texas. The crews of the 381st often stated that Pyote was "right in the middle of nowhere." The first crews to arrive at the training site found dirt, sand, high winds and roaming cattle. Afternoons at Pyote usually meant the arrival of sand storms and the aircraft were usually sent out on training flights to avoid these storms.

Africa while in the Pacific there was as yet no definite trend towards using the B-24 rather than the B-17.

Bombing and gunnery practice, with bombs being provided often at the expense of the 96th BG and the latter sometimes at the expense of the local cattle, steadily increased. Dust storms continued to be the major hazard but the ultimate benefit of the sustained pressure of training was apparent later when thirty-six aircraft formations were flown on a regular basis.

On 25 February, a practice mission to Wilcox Dry Lake, Arizona officially completed the first phase of training and 2nd Air Force duly authorized phase two. This period involved more squadron and group formation flying over greater ranges with considerable pressure on ground crews to achieve high aircraft availability rates. Their labors produced an 80 percent minimum average. On 31 March preparations were made to transfer to Pueblo with movement four days later. New B-17s, ten per squadron, were assigned. These aircraft had new brakes with 58 inch tires and, of more relevance to future operations, forward-firing flexible gun mounts in the nose. This increased armament was deemed vital to help ward off head-on attacks by Luftwaffe fighters.

The emphasis on missions over Germany increased during practice briefings, a clear hint of the Group's destination. Other indicators of where the group was bound were the dropping of Japanese aircraft from recognition classes and ground crew training now reflecting European conditions. Allocation of the B-17s intended to be taken into action was made at Pueblo; a grand total of forty-one were ultimately involved with

B-17F Flying Fortresses of the 381st Bomb Group on the ramp at either Pyote, Texas or Pueblo, Colorado during the Spring of 1943. The group worked up at Pyote during the Winter and Spring of 1943 before moving to Pueblo.

LT Reinhard King's crew "hard at work" during Phase 1 training at Pyote, Texas with their aircraft, HELLS ANGEL, in the background. Both aircraft and crew were declared Missing In Action (MIA) on 17 August 1943 during the Schweinfurt raid, although crew survived as POWs.

one being passed to the 94th BG and one being left behind. What was at first a collection of characterless machines soon took on personality in the form of names, polite and otherwise. Before long, a Fort was referred to not by its number but as *Tinkertoy*, *The Joker*, *Georgia Rebel* and so on.

Overseas movement was daily anticipated and confirmation came on 2 May when the first advanced party moved out for Atlantic City, New Jersey. On 12 May 1943, they flew by C-54 to Prestwick, Scotland. Aircraft dispatch commenced on 4 May when the CO flew to Salinas, Kansas, with the Group following over the next forty-eight hours. LT Marvin Lord's aircraft lost a main gear wheel on takeoff but managed to get aloft and headed for Oklahoma City as ordered, since a repair depot was located there. He was able to make a successful crash-landing and the aircraft was later repaired. The Pueblo base staff had watched the errant wheel bounce down the runway but their efforts to retrieve it were in vain and it was of academic interest to Lord's crew.

The first aircraft departing Salinas for England took off on 15 May and five days later COL Nazzaro was in position at Bovingdon where he was quickly joined by the other crews. There they would receive orientation lectures prior to moving to Ridgewell. The ground crew's progress was much more stately. Between 9 and 26 May they transferred from Pueblo to Camp Killmer, NJ, where a fourteen day stay ended with embarkation on the mighty QUEEN MARY and an Atlantic crossing, which was completed on 1 June at Greenock, Scotland. The final lap to Ridgewell was made by railroad train.

Ridgewell was known as Army Air Force Station 167 and was situated near the Essex/Suffolk border. Although the towns of Braintree, Halstead and Haverhill lay within a few miles, civilization, to its new occupiers. was London. London was at least two hours away by "Toonerville Trolley." American parlance for the miniature rail stock and cramped compartments of the LNER service.

Airfield layout was typical, with two T2 pattern hangars and thirty-six (later fifty) dispersal pans. The main runway was 2,000 yards long on an East/West axis with two secondary runways 1,400 yards long making up a triangular pattern. Main support facilities were grouped around the hangar south of the main runway, while other working and living sites were in a valley further to the south and concealed from the flight lines. Nissen and pre-fabricated huts were provided; in short, Ridgewell was a typical base, familiar to countless crews whose lot it was to fly and maintain heavy bombers in wartime England.

The bombers arrived on 9 June, and a week later, forty-four of the forty-five assigned aircraft were standing alert, ready for combat.

1943

The Hard Road To Schweinfurt

As with all "freshman" units, the 381st BG was allotted a "diversionary" task for its first mission. On 22 June, the combat crews were briefed to attack the Ford and General Motors plant at Antwerp in company with the equally untried 384th BG. This effort was expected to draw enemy attention away from the main 8th AAF thrust at the Huls/Recklinghausen synthetic oil plant. Full fighter escort cover could be provided for what was a short run across the channel. To those assembled in the briefing room it must have seemed only yesterday they had sat through "mock" briefing sessions back in the States, perhaps a little sleepy and bored. But here they listened and listened hard to every word — school was over.

Flying with the 381st BG was BGEN Frank 0. Hunter, head of the 8th Fighter Command, who was riding as an observer in a B-17F (42-30024) flown by LT Withers. There were no "aborts" among the twenty bombers dispatched. For the first time, over what would be twenty-two months, the local population heard the initially ragged series of coughing, sputtering motors blend into a constant dinning roar followed by constant squealing of brakes as the bombers taxied to the runway. At 0709 the first B-17 eased its way onto the runway and ten minutes later all twenty were airborne.

The sight of B-17s assembling into their distinctive formations would later become familiar to those below. Sadly, they would also become accustomed to seeing depleted and scattered formations easing into the airfield circuit after rough missions, flares popping from aircraft with dead or wounded aboard and forced landings that did not always have a happy outcome. Link-up with the 384th BG was made without difficulty. The attack plan called for the 381st BG to fly in "trail" to the 384th BG and progress was made to North Foreland where a direct course to Antwerp was set. The anticipated rendezvous with the fighter escort never occurred, since a message to its commander advising him that the bombers were forty minutes behind schedule had not been received. The B-17 crews searched vainly for the "Little Friends" while COL Peaslee

BGEN Frank O, Hunter, commander of the 8th Fighter Command flew in LT Withers' B-17F (42-30024) for the 381st Bomb Group's first bombing mission over Europe, an attack against the Ford and General Motors plants in Antwerp, on 22 June 1943

CAPT Bob Shank's *Linda Mary* of the 533rd BS, suffered a runaway propeller on the Group's first mission over Europe. The aircraft was named for CAPT Shank's baby daughter and went on to fly seventeen missions and claim six German fighters before the crew posed for a group picture on 17 December 1943.

Little Chuck brought home LT Inman Jobe's crew to a 'hairy' crash-landing on their first mission. A concrete post sliced off the left wing at the wing root but miraculously none of the crew was injured. The B-17F was scrapped following its brief but eventful combat career.

balanced the possible heavy loss to his small unescorted formation against the loss of diversionary benefit to the Huls raiders. He decided to press on and hope the escorts would link up before enemy airspace was penetrated. As the target was being closed, there were hopes that a "milkrun" mission was on the cards — a hope dashed by the unannounced arrival of the Luftwaffe from a "twelve o'clock level" angle. The initial assault was so sudden that gunners were largely unable to bring their weapons to bear upon the Fw 190s. No bombers were downed in the first attack but LT Shenk's *LINDA MARY* soon developed a runaway propeller and LT Jobe's *LITTLE CHUCK* also lost its No 2 engine. As the bomb run was begun, one B-17 (probably LT Horr's) was knocked out of formation and crashed in Belgium, while LT Martin's aircraft was reported to have crashed into the sea along with a pursuing FW on the way out from the target. The Allied fighter cover arrived just after bombs away. The bombing was reasonably accurate, bombs having been deliberately under-aimed to avoid over-shooting

onto the surrounding civilian housing. By this point both Ridgewell "cripples" were on their own and under severe attack. Jobe still had his bombs on board and was nearly back across the Channel before they were finally jettisoned. In addition, he had to fly on elevators and automatic pilot alone. Finally, after being picked up by the P-47 escort, No 3 engine caught fire and died over the English coast. As if this was not enough, as the bomber was put down on its belly, it careered into a concrete post which miraculously sliced off the left wing at its root without the expected explosive result — none of the crew were injured.

Shenk's crew were reported MIA by the returning crews but despite several injured men, including SGT Brinton who later died, *LINDA MARY* staggered back to a more sedate crash-landing on the South English coast. She was brought back into service and was regularly used until her loss on 6 March 1944, the last "original" bomber to be lost.

Two bombers and their crews were Missing In Action (MIA), one bomber was declared "Category E" and two returning crewmen were fatally injured. This was a sharp introduction to what was known as

This scene of devastation at the 533rd BS dispersal is the aftermath of a bomb loading accident on B-17F 42-30024. The explosion snuffed out the lives of twenty-three Americans. The incident occurred on 23 June 1943, the day after the aircraft had carried GEN Hunter on his observation mission over Antwerp.

Intelligence officers debriefing crews after their return from one of the Group's early missions. The officer sitting against the wall is the Group Commanding Officer, LCOL Joe J. Nazzaro. His promotion to full "Bird" Colonel occurred after the Group's arrival in England.

"The Big League of Sky Fighting." An even tougher potential task awaited the crews three days later, Hamburg, where COL Nazzaro led twenty-four bombers to strike the Klockner Aero plant. Solid cloud cover resulted in only fourteen aircraft releasing on target, while LT Schrader (42-30027) was lost along with CAPT Hamilton (533rd BS Operations Officer). The second mission had actually been briefed but "aborted" on 23 June. This same day was notable for a shocking type of ground accident which would recur at several bomber bases during the Second World War. Bombs were being hoisted into position in 42-30024 (which GEN Hunter had flown to Antwerp just twenty-four hours earlier) and some ground and combat crew were clustered around and inside the 533rd BS bomber when, at 1100 there was a rush of air and the B-17 erupted in flames and smoke. A deathly pause of forty-five sec-

The 381st Bomb Group's first medal winner was T/SGT John Sinclair, who was presented with America's third highest award, the Silver Star, by COL Nazzaro on 21 August 1943. T/SGT Sinclair was badly wounded but attended to other wounded crew members as well as manning several gun positions. He flew with CAPT Shank on *Linda Mary*.

onds ended with a second explosion which, in one witness' stated, "blew the ship off the face of the earth". A total of twenty-one U.S.personnel and one British civilian were killed instantly. It later transpired the bomb fuses were already in position, so a dropped bomb was the likely cause. A B-17 (42-29992) in the adjacent dispersal was so badly damaged she was "scrapped"; LT Tull, working in her nose was struck in the head by metal fragments and killed. The poor 533rd BS personnel must have felt "jinxed" at this early stage — five aircraft destroyed or crashed and over forty men MIA or killed in a mere seventy-two hours.

June was closed off with an "abortive" run to Villacoublay and while the 28th and 29th runs to St Nazaire's U-boat pens and Triqueville airfield were made.

By July of 1943, the VIII Bomber Command's strength stood at twelve Groups, which were able to despatch around 300 bombers. The POINTBLANK directive of 10 June switched target priority to the German aircraft industry, particularly the sectors producing fighters. It was realized that if Allied fighters and heavy bombers could destroy the main opposition to the European Air Offensive as soon as possible, then the invasion of the Continent would be an immeasurably easier task. Bomber attacks on French air depots and airfields heralded the start of POINTBLANK. Le Mans (4th), Villacoublay (10th) and Amiens-Glissey (14th) were the Group's contribution. On the latter mission, three crews experienced the fortunes of war in different fashion. During Group assembly LT Hedin's *RED HOT RIDING HOOD* (42-3223) started smoking in its No 3 engine. T/SGT Potts suggested it be "feathered" shortly before he called, "ooops, its gone!" The next thing Potts knew, he was hanging in mid-air, his B-17 having been split in two by the rogue propeller torn from No 3 engine. Potts watched the final death throes of the bomber; it flattened out at around 6,000 feet, the outer wing sections detached themselves and the nose section folded back over the truncated fuselage. Only three other crewmen survived, one of whom (LT Frank Cappel) was unconscious for days and later medically discharged the service. The 533rd BS bomber fell on and around Rattlesden airfield.

LT Holdom flying *WIDGET* (42-30011) was lost over the target area with all ten men killed. After leaving the target, The FW 190s of JG2 kept up their assault from head-on (one of their leaders, Hans Georg Eder, being a pioneer of this deadly method of attack). One FW was struck by return fire from LT Bob Black, the bombardier on Ed Manchester's *TS* (42-3211). Careering on in at a vertical angle the errant fighter provided LT Bob Weniger with a horrifying split-second view of its left wing impacting between the Fortress' fuselage and its No 3 engine. Cart wheeling over the wing, the FW fell away leaving the B-17 with a shattered engine cowling, a hole in the vertical fin and damage to the left stabilizer. Although a remarkably small degree of damage in the circumstances, the impact almost stalled out *TS*, which, but for magnificent recovery action between the pilots, would almost certainly crashed. Now detached from the Group, Manchester and Whenever brought TS home under steady fighter attack. The attacks were finally beaten off by P-47s of the 78th FG (including CAPT London, the first 8th fighter Ace). A final hazard of barrage balloons around Manston airfield was negotiated and the Fort made a safe belly-landing. A subsequent check of the airframe disclosed a cannon barrel from the FW nestling in the bomb-bay. It was, in Bob Weniger's words, "one hell of a hard way to bring down the Luftwaffe."

In the face of such fierce and sustained opposition, USAAF bomber crews strove to complete their mandatory twenty-five missions and earn rotation back to the States. With average losses approaching ten percent, at this time, there was a better chance of a cancer victim surviving his illness, than a combat crewman surviving his tour. The last week in July committed the 8th to a closely-spaced series of missions thereafter known as Blitz Week. A deceptively easy start was made on 24 July when 1st Wing struck the Nordiske-Lettmetal aluminum plant at Heroya, while 4th Wing went further up Norway to Trondheim. This was the

This 381st B-17F (42-30020) made a belly landing at AAF Station 167 (Ridgewell) on arrival in England. The aircraft letter (N) is carried above the serial, most Groups carried theirs below the serial prior to the introduction of Group insignia and identification letters.

first time use was made of Splasher Beacons (British-made medium frequency units based in East Anglia) to assist Group and Wing assembly in overcast weather. An unusually low target approach was made at 2,500 feet until shortly before the attack when the twin forces scaled the stratosphere — a tactic which seemingly fooled the enemy radar system since resistance was confined to "meager" flak over Heroya where the newly commissioned plant was completely destroyed. The flak was hardly "meager" for LT Osce V. Jones in *GEORGIA REBEL* (42-3217) because his crippled B-17 was forced to head for neutral Sweden, the first USAAF aircraft to do so. It was also the only 1st Wing loss that day.

The Norwegian milkrun was brutally contrasted with Hamburg the next day when the Klockner Aero plant was again assigned for assault. **This is *TS* of the 535th BS bearing original squadron codes on the fuselage which were changed after a few weeks of operations to MS. She was scrapped after limping back to a crash-landing at Manston on 14 July 1943, after surviving a head-on collision with a Fw 190 which nearly caused a fatal stall. Copilot Bob Weniger was from Texas, but *TS* did not stand for "Texas State", it really stood for "Tough S..t."**

Assembly problems, which left the 381st BG well behind the other two Combat Bomb Wing (CBW) units, was followed by six bombers, including the designated Leader "aborting." CAPT George Shackley (Deputy Lead) took over but failed to close the gap. Smoke from the previous night's RAF raid obscured the target and the sixteen bombers turned for home, holding their loads until a rail junction at Heide near the coast was chosen as a "target of opportunity". They had left 42-30013/*LETHAL LADY* (LT Moore) and 42-29976 (LT J Owen) behind as flak and fighter victims, while a third 532nd BS crew, led by CAPT Joe Alexander was forced to turn back over the coast by a "runaway" propeller and had to seek a crash-landing . All but four of the thirty crewmen on the lost B-17s survived as POWS.

Barely had the engines had time to cool and the ground crews time to patch up and repair their charges, when the call to again attack Hamburg came. Twenty-two bombardiers were prevented, by smoke,from sighting on the Blohm und Voss shipyards and a diversion to the Howaldtswerke U-boat yards had to be made. A day's respite was followed by three consecutive runs to Altenbuna, Kiel and Kassel (28-30 July). The first senior rank loss was suffered at Kassel when MAJ Bob Post (532nd BS commander, who had been promoted from CAPT on 27 July) went down with LT Humason in 42-3100. A successful crash-landing had a dismal sequel for Bob because he suffered a broken leg and loss of one eye when the stranded bomber was strafed by an FW.190; in fact he was repatriated the following year. In addition to the four B-17s lost, the

CHUG-A-LUG LuLu was 42-3225 of the 535th BS which took LT Loren Disbrow's crew to Schweinfurt on 17 August 1943. The Fortress was fatally crippled and eventually abandoned over Belgium on the way home. No less than four of the crew succeeded in evading capture and returned to England. There are four White Swaztikas on the nose for enemy fighter kills.

Another "original" Group B-17F was Strato Sam (42-3092) of the 533rd BS. She was one of eleven aircraft declared as MIA on the first Schweinfurt raid when the Group suffered the highest unit losses. The nose-mounted gun was meant to combat head-on fighter attacks, but it was found to be insufficient to halt determined Luftwaffe attacks.

534th BS' *WHALETAIL* (42-3221) was flown to a desperate forced-landing in a Norfolk field by LT Bill Wroblicka, after successive power loss in three engines.

Although the week's effort had resulted in some accurate bomb-strikes, the overall policy of hitting a number of targets with small forces rather than making a combined strike at one target, tended to minimize the extent of the damage. Also, more use of incendiaries was needed since precision machinery was more susceptible to fire distortion than to blast effects.

Blitz Week had taken a high toll of bombers from among the 8th's overall strength, so the scale of operations in early August was accordingly low. The authorities; however, were also building up for a special mission that was to be launched against two key industrial targets; their names would become synonymous with unescorted daylight bombing — Schweinfurt and Regensburg. It was 12 August before the 8th ventured into Europe to hit the Ruhr. Up to this day, the 534th BS had not lost any bombers in combat but that happy situation was altered when LT Wroblicka in *DEVIL'S ANGEL* (42-29954) went down along with LT Moon in *MARGIE MAE* (42-5847) and LT Evans flying *FORGET ME NOT* (42-29950). Two "milk runs" to Vlissengen (15th) and Le

Bourget (16th) was the easy prelude to one of the most momentous missions in the Second World War for the 8th and the 381st BG .

The planners of the USAAF's part of the Combined Bombing Offensive were continually seeking "bottle-neck" targets which, if knocked out, would materially help to "shorten the war." Ball-bearings were regarded as essential to Germany's industrial effort — knock out the main production plant at Schweinfurt and the war effort would literally grind to a halt. A novel refinement of the plan of attack was for the 4th Wing to go in on the Messerschmitt plant at Regensburt ten minutes ahead of the 1st Wing force headed for Schweinfurt. The intention was to split the German fighter strength; also the 4th Wing would fly on to North Africa rather than head back to England. Allied fighter cover still only extended to the boundary of Germany so every move to ward off the worst effects of the Luftwaffe had to be used.

That this daring plan did not work was due to several factors. Fog held both Wings on the ground at the briefed take-off time but, although the 4th Wing was forced to launch one hour later in order to reach North Africa in daylight, the lst Wing was still held back until weather conditions cleared. The later take-off also "meant a change in target approach over featureless countryside as well as a down-wind bomb-run". Tactical maneuvers by the Wing Commander, COL Gross, would add to the crews problems.

All this was still ahead of the twenty-six Ridgewell crews taking part as they assembled around noon under MAJ Hall. The Group was in the low position within the 101 PCBW with six bombers assigned to the Composite Group flying in the high position. The Luftwaffe had ample

MSGT Fitzgerald's ground crew team stand by *Forget Me Not II* on 18 August 1943. The B-17F carried some very appropriate artwork. MSGT Fitzgerald would become the Division's leading crew chief with a total of 169 non-aborted missions. The Fortress was lost on 9 October 1943 with LT Herbert Carqueville in command.

The letter L on the tail of *OLD COFFINS* is its individual identification letter and not a Group/Bomb Division identification. The Group marking was introduced in early July and was carried in a triangle on vertical fin and right wingtip. *OLD COFFINS* was transferred to 305th BG on 22 August and returned to the States in the Spring of 1944.

This B-17F Fortress of the 532nd Bomb Squadron was at Ridgewell for only ten days before going down on the Kassel raid of 30 July 1943 during Blitz Week. The aircraft's co-pilot was the squadron commander, MAJ Bob Post. The aircraft letter/number on the fin was an unusual variation.

The shattered tailplane of RED HOT RIDING HOOD, a B-17F of the 533rd BS of lies within the perimeter of Rattlesden airfield. The aircraft disintegrated during group assembly for a mission on 14 July 1943 and only four crewmen survived.

time to sortie against the Regensburg raiders, then land, re-arm and re-fuel to take on the approaching 1st Wing B-17s. Their initial assaults came in even before the P-47s and Spitfires turned for home. What then ensued was one of the most bloody and costly air battles of the Second World War. For fully three hours, the bombers would be under heavy or intermittent fighter assault. Waves of FW 190s and Messerschmitts, heading in almost exclusively from "Twelve O'clock level" poured in overwhelming firepower which the largely unsighted American gunners could barely respond to. Casualties soon began to mount.

For the 381st BG, two 534th BS bombers (LT Simpson's *LUCKY LADY* [42-30245] and LT Forkner's 42-3227) were downed over Belgium. The Group's exposed low position attracted particular enemy attention as the bombers bore into Germany. In quick succession, LT Neil Wright in *SWEET LE LANI* (42-30028), Flight Officer Hudson in STRATO SAM (42-3092) and LT Painter in *KING MALFUNCTION II* (42-30140) were culled from the Group ranks, closely followed by LT Atkinson's 42-29983. The Group's losses continued around Frankfurt with LT Reinhart King's *HELL'S ANGEL* (42-29978) grievously damaged and salvoing its bombs as her crew took to their parachutes. As Schweinfurt was being crossed, for what was an overall poor bombing result. The B-17s of LT Harry Smith and LT Leo Jarvis were fading and now fell away - Jarvis recalls doing a slow roll to clear the formation — and all twenty crewmen jumped . Of the nine aircraft lost so far, seven were from the main Group and two from the Composite unit. Turning

West, the crews had a welcome respite of some sixty minutes from regular attack — probably the German fighters had anticipated a similar Southern course as with 4th Wing -- but as the Rhine was reached the assaults began again in full fury. LT Disbrow's *CHUGALUG LULU* (42-3225) had been straggling most of the way from Schweinfurt and steadily losing altitude, but as Belgium was appearing under the ailing bomber's wings she was finally abandoned west of Eupen where 1st Wing's lonely battle had commenced. Ten bombers were cut from the Group strength as the Channel was traversed but the defenders efforts were about to claim an eleventh victim. LT Darrow had also been straggling even before Schweinfurt but, unlike LT Disbrow, his B-17 was kept fairly close to the PCBW. His effort to gain English shores failed a few miles short and 42-29735 was eased into the Channel waters with all ten men soon being picked up by an RAF rescue launch. Eighty-five of Darrow's colleagues had not been so lucky, although only five were actually killed while eleven evaded capture.

The 381st BG bore the dubious "distinction" of bearing the highest unit losses within 1st Wing, although its companion 91st BG had only one less loss. In all thirty-six bombers went down along with twenty-four from 4th Wing — a stunning manner in which to celebrate the 8th's first full year of combat. For many of the Ridgewell crews the chances

Margie Mae came from a small Vega B-17F production group on which the cheek gun mountings were reversed, while the left fitting was bulged and un-framed. The bomber's scoreboard shows credit for nine misions and one enemy aircraft. The Fortress was one of three declared MIA after a 12 Aug 1943 raid on Ruhr targets. The pilot on that mission was LT Moon.

Leo Jarvis (second from left, front) was declared Missing In Action (MIA) on the first Schweinfurt raid. Apart from LT Bill Lockhart (right, front) who lost an eye, all the other crew members were captured uninjured and spent the rest of the war as POWs. The aircraft was 42-29731 of 534th BS while crew was attached to the 532nd BS.

Lucky crew, lucky aircraft. THE JOKER was the regular mount for LT Will Baltrusaitus (532nd BS) and his crew. The aircraft survived some forty-five missions prior to honorable retirement back to the United States in April of 1944.

of completing 25 missions now seemed slimmer than ever; more than half the "original" crews were gone in just eight weeks of combat. For the 8th, the prospect of the "self-defending bomber" theory standing up to Luftwaffe expertise was a fast fading one, but one which still had to face its final and even crueler test in October.

The general mood of depression that evening was such that the need to declare a "non-operational" state was actively discussed. This had to be balanced against the danger of morale being equally affected if crews were stood down and allowed to dwell upon matters. Therefore when a mission to Gilze Rijen was called for on 19 August the group provided at least a token force. Adding weight to the truism "there are no easy missions" was the loss of LT Koenig's crew in 42-3101 (this crew had been the "model" training crew for the 535th BS in the States).

With a good proportion of the 8th's strength resting on another continent for upwards of seven days and the mauling handed out to lst Wing, it was not surprising that target choice was accordingly restricted to close-range locations for the remainder of August. Only thirty -six bombers in all were dispatched from Ridgewell for its three missions in the month's last eight days which reflected the pace of aircraft and crew replenishment. The attack on 27 August was interesting since it was one of the first against a yet unknown menace — launch sites for the V-1 flying bomb, which would be operational in June of 1944 and cause much damage in southeast England.

By 3 September, SGTs Ed Myers (ROG) and Charles Bang (Gunner) were veteran crewmen on LT Chapman's team. Why they were assigned to fly with LT Ben Zum's "rookie" crew is unknown. They were among nine of the surviving men abandoning the 532nd BS's *BIG TIME OPERATOR* (42-29789) over Romilly-sur-Seine that day. Coming to earth near some civilians, Ed was motioned to take cover in nearby woods where he remained for two days. During this time he was visited by two children to whom he made the potentially fatal move of responding to their chatter with the word "Ja", despite knowing no German: Getting no further response from the populace, he set out. Despite escape lecture orders not to do so, he walked through a town main street and along a railroad track (for which the penalty was shooting on sight!) before being picked up by a cyclist — who had no problem recognizing Ed for what he was since he was still wearing his G.I. coveralls. Moved in quick succession to several houses, he spent time in Paris but by the month's end was in Brest, his disguise being that of a deaf and dumb umbrella-maker. Here he joined no less than forty other Allied evaders first in a bakery and then for six uncomfortable days incarcerated in the smelly hold of a fishing boat. The vessel was given a

This B-17F Fortress became group's first "hangar queen" after it made a belly landing on 9 June. The aircraft has already been stripped of its armament, outer wing panels, engines, vertical and horizontal stabilizers and fuselage sections. These parts went to repair other battle damaged B-17s within the group.

This B-17F arrived on 16 June 43 as a replacement, probably for 42-30020 of the 532nd BS. The bomber lasted until 4 Mar 1944 when she was declared Missing In Action (MIA) on the second Berlin mission. The VE squadron codes are still to be applied. The 532nd was the only one among the four 381st BG squadrons not to change its codes.

WHALETAIL ended her combat career in a Norfolk wheatfield where she was put down by LT Bill Wroblicka on 29 July 1943 after the Fortress lost power in three engines. Two weeks later Wroblicka's entire crew was shot down and became POWs.

cursory check by Wehrmacht guards on 24 October and the crew took her to sea . Evading German controls, crew and evaders reached SW England some two days later. Ed's safe arrival back was not many days ahead of LT Bob Neslon and SGT Ray Genz. This duo had bailed out of LT Painter's stricken B-17 near Munstereifel on 17 August. From this German region, they had steadily worked their way back into Occupied Europe where they made contact with the Resistance, who spirited the airmen through France and into neutral Spain.

The mission of 6 September was another set-back for the 8th when forty-five B-17s were lost off a cloud-thwarted run on Stuttgart's ball-bearing facilities. Eighteen of the losses were to ditchings in the Channel — the result of lingering too long in the target area. Ridgewell's losses were nil but CAPT Dexter Lishon was hard pressed to make it back to England where he put *WHALETAIL II* down in a field. The bomber was put back into service and was fated to out-last Lishon's time with the 381st BG by some two months.

Once again the 8th metaphorically "drew in its claws" by going for targets in France and the Low Countries and the 381st BG took part in six of these raids. The final month's mission; however, was to Emden in northwestern Germany where the first use of the blind-bombing aid H2X was made. With an average circular error of some two miles there was little hope of good bomb concentrations but at least some pressure was kept up on the German war effort. The mission was also notable since P-47s were able to cover the bombers as far as the target thanks to the availability of larger-sized external fuel tanks. Grateful as the bomber crews were for this extended protection there was an awareness among their ranks that salvation on deep-penetration missions would primarily depend upon their gunners for the foreseeable future. They must have also known in their hearts that the September run of missions was only a respite before making full-strength thrusts into Central Europe.

Black Week

On 23 June 1943 this B-17F was severely damaged during the bomb-loading explosion that destroyed 42-30024 and was declared as salvage some nine days later. The OQ unit codes for the 533rd BS were later changed to VP.

Many of the combat crewmen filing into the briefing room on 8 October had flown to Emden (2 October) and Frankfurt (4 October and, neither mission had resulted in losses. Two of the pilots, CAPT Lishon and Manchester, were close friends and Manchester's copilot Bob Weniger was to ride as tail gunner/observer in the Lead bomber. At the other end of the experience-scale was LT Ed Klein, who was on his first mission. The bombers assigned were a similar mix of veteran and new aircraft and today's mission would further enhance *TINKERTOY*'s controversial reputation.

Group and Wing assembly were made without incident and enemy fighter attacks did not cause many problems as the coast was crossed and up to the Initial Point. It was from this stage on that, according to LT Weniger, "all hell broke loose" and the events of "Black Friday" began to unfold. Turning right off the target, the Group came within range of Bremen's formidable flak belt. A close burst shattered *OUR MOM*'s (42-29832) nose, causing fragments of glass to strike Ed Klein's face. Upon clearing his vision, he was astonished to see open sky where before there had been B-17s. Wondering if LT Miller (P) was off course he called him only to be told "look downwards." what he saw was numerous B-17s falling or struggling, obviously in distress. *OUR MOM*, on its own now, attempted to close with another two stragglers only to be attacked by fighters, which killed SGT Klugee and almost blew the rudder off its mounting. Realizing by now that the stragglers they were closing on were equally, if not more crippled, Miller climbed towards a larger formation ahead of them and came home safely.

One of the B-17s Ed had seen in trouble was Bill Cormany's lead ship with MAJ Ingenhutt (535th BS Commander) on board. In the tail, Bob Weniger recalled shrapnel rattling against the fuselage and the B-17 being buffeted by close flak bursts. The pilots continued to lead as far as the breakaway point even though the No 2 engine was on fire. Cormany now dived in an attempt to extinguish the blaze but the action only blew off the engine cowling . With flames threatening to break through the firewall protecting the inner fuel tanks, the bomber was pulled out

GEORGIA REBEL of the 535th BS parked on her dispersal pad in England. This Fortress earned the dubious distinction of being the first USAAF aircraft to divert to Sweden (24 July 1943). She was flown by LTs Osce V. Jones and George Mackintosh, who later returned to England only to be shot down on separate missions and taken as Prisoners Of War (POWs).

Sweet Le Lani was a 534th BS "original" aircraft which lasted until 17 Aug 1943. The aircraft was assigned to LT Neil Wright and his crew. Besides the tasty artwork below the cockpit, the Fortress carried four mission symbols under the navigator's gun position

The crew of the *Joker* pose in front of their aircraft duringt the Summer of 1943. Baltrusaitus is second from right at front while to his right is LT Arthur Sample who later was assigned his own crew (which were declared MIA on 8 October). Standing (L-R) are SGTs Murphy, Thorpe, Pease, McGaughy, Acquilino and Hone. Sample was the sole fatality.

around 17,000 feet and the bale-out order was given.

CAPT Manchester's TS II (42-29941) banked right to avoid Cormany's aircraft but must have been disabled because he soon disappeared with fire in one engine and in the fuselage. Survivors among the crew spoke of the nose being blown in and finally the bomber broke in two, carrying Manchester and CAPT Jukes (535th Ops Officer) to their deaths. In the severed tail, SGTs Berk and McCook spiraled down to a miraculous safe landing at Talge, where their pilot and four other men were interred. Two 532nd BS bombers *OLE FLAK SACK* (42-29854) and *FEATHER MERCHANT* (42-30009) fell almost simultaneously. The former under LT Baltrusaitus' former co-pilot (LT Sample) went out of control and exploded with only two survivors. LT Jack Pry and seven men got out while their B-17 crashed near Diepoltz, as did Sample's aircraft. The sole lost crew to survive intact was CAPT Lishon's in *BOBBY T* (42-30722). Details on the remaining two losses were unclear for LT Kemp in 42-3123 and LT Hartje in *NIP AND TUCK* (42-29765), although Hartje did survive.

Seven aircraft lost was grim enough, but the incident most indelibly imprinted on returning crewmen's minds was what happened to LT Hal Minerich. Seeing bombers go down was sobering, but the often grisly details were rarely known until after the war. *TINKERTOY* came home with stark evidence of what could happen to a man if fate decreed. Under fighter attack, the B-17 took a burst which ripped off the nose canopy and penetrated the windscreen . Minerich was decapitated and blood pumping from his body sprayed and instantly froze into a slick all over the cockpit. Copilot LT Thomas Sellars was wounded by the exploding shells but with assistance from T/SGT Miller made it home with *TINKERTOY* ground-looping on landing. Sellars was later awarded the Distinguished Service Cross, one of only two won by 381st BG personnel.

Total 8th AF losses over Bremen were thirty aircraft of which almost twenty-five percent came from Ridgewell while enemy aircraft claims by group gunners was twenty-five destroyed reflecting the air battle's intensity. Small wonder the group was to receive what would be the first of its two Distinguished Unit Citations.

Next day, the Group put up sixteen bombers for a long mission to Ankiam's Arado plant in Prussia. Crossing in and out over the North Baltic coast would, in the planners opinion, prevent mass enemy fighter reaction until the bombers were well on their way home. The crews were not so confident and in some cases stocked up with more than the permitted maximum of 10,000 rounds of ammunition. In LT Gleichaufl's case this almost proved fatal. Unknown to him the carefully stacked extra rounds in the radio room were distributed aft and even

The Summer weather in England could sometimes be very pleasant as on 1 Aug 1943. Ground crewmen are changing an outer wing section using inflatable airbags to raise the replacement unit into place.

B-17s of the 381st BG form up for what is probably a practice mission in early 1943. Three elements of the box formation are in position but rear element still needs to be tightened up.

worse, the tail gunner took up his position at take-off! The bomber barely staggered off the runway then headed inexorably for the ground. Quick reaction in lowering the wheels and literally "bouncing" the B-17 off what was a fortuitously open and dry patch of soil saved the day from what should have been certain death for all on board. Bomber and crew would return from Anklam but not so Gleichaufl's Commanding Officer, MAJ Landon Hendricks. This superb leader was flying in 42-30012 and leading his 533rd BS.

Contrary to expectations, fighter interception was experienced early on and sustained right up to the point where the Group crossed out over the Danish coast upon withdrawal. As Denmark was passing below Hendricks was seen to lower his wheels as a sign for the deputy lead to take over, whereupon he dropped back and out of formation to be promptly set on and downed by several Fw 190s. Some returning crewmen suggested at debriefing that he might have ditched, but sadly none of his crew were ever found and their names are inscribed on the "Wall of the Missing" at Madingley Cemetery, Cambridge. Also recorded there is LT Carqueville who was flying *FORGET ME NOT II* (42-3180). The trio of Anklam losses was completed by LT Loftin's *BAT-TLIN BOMB SPRAYER* (42-29958).

For the other three officers and the engineer abandoning a fourth B-17, it seemed their action was justified because the pilot, LT Doug Winters, was assumed to have been killed by cannon shells which had impacted in the cockpit area. In fact, he had only been temporarily stunned and as his hazy vision cleared he witnessed the four men's departure with one of them quickly standing to attention and saluting Winters before baling out. The worthy lieutenant, being far from dead, put the aircraft on auto-pilot to go back and extinguish a fire before resuming his position

LT Darrow's crew were debriefed after their ditching in the English Channel. The Fortress went down after receiving battle damage during the Schweinfurt mission on 17 Aug 1943. At least two of the crew are wearing RAF battledress.

LT Bob Nelson not only baled out of LT Painter's *KING MALFUNCTION II* (42-30140) but succeeded, along with SGT Genz, in evading capture and returning to England within two months. Bob received the Silver Star from COL Reid (Ground Executive Officer) on 20 Dec 1943.

and guiding the Fortress back to Ridgewell (available records do not indicate how many crew actually jumped but the ground crew must have been surprised at the lower number of men coming out than had embarked.)

Ten B-17s lost in two consecutive missions was a very poor omen for the 10 October run to Monster and only seven aircraft were despatched as part of the 1st CBW strength of thirty-three, barely half of whom actually got sortie "credit". The city center was the designated aiming point which was a stark departure from American policy of selecting purely industrial sources for attack at least at this stage of the Second World War. Happily for the group all aircraft returned, the 13th CBW suffered twenty-five of the thirty bombers lost this day.

Four days later, the briefing map ribbons stretched to a target the 381st BG never wanted to see again — Schweinfurt. Shock was registered as well not only as regards the target but also at the Group drawing the CBW Low position. This mission was a "maximum effort" by the 8th to finally knock out the vital ball-bearing factories located there. Tragically, as with Schweinfurt/Regensburg on 17 August ,the German fighters and flak would decimate the bomber ranks by over sixty aircraft. The 381st BG had led the casualty list on that occasion, but today Lady Luck would smile on its crews. The Group was late in assembling and MAJ George Shackley decided to cut for the English coast in order to pick up the 1st CBW. This was achieved, but to his surprise (and probable relief at avoiding this '"Purple Heart" sector in any CBW) the Low position was already occupied by a similarly affected Group from the Lead 40th CBW who had tacked onto the 1st CBW's vacant formation slot. Shackley pulled the 381st BG up level with the high squadron, which was leading the 1st CBW and the expanded formation headed

The HELLION flies over a typical East Anglian countryside. The national insignia had a Red surround and the Group practice of carrying the individual aircraft letter on the tail instead of the fuselage is revealed.

The nose art on The HELLION featured what appeared to be a hellish wolf. The Fortress was transferred to the RAF during early 1944 to serve with No 214 (Radio Counter Measures) Squadron .

out. When the enemy fighters struck from both flanks of the bomber stream just past Aachen, they appeared to concentrate on the hapless Low Group (305th BG from Chelveston). By the time the bomb-run commenced, only three of its fifteen B-17s remained and one of these fell just after bombs away. In sharp contrast, only LT Yorba in 42-29803 (ironically an ex-305th BG Fortress) failed to come home to Ridgewell. "Black Thursday." as this day came to be christened, was a water-shed since it spelled the final demise of the "self-defending bomber" theory although the writing had been on the wall for some months from Blitz Week onward.

The remainder of 1943 was to involve the 8th in retrenchment and build-up for a revived and hopefully decisive offensive in 1944. For the 381st BG, the rest of October was relatively peaceful with a pair of missions briefed on the 18th and 20th but scrubbed, as the bombers were outward bound over the North Sea and Belgium respectively; however sortie "credit" was granted for the latter effort when the 534th BS was allocated to the 306th BG's High Squadron slot. Two weeks passed before the next call came for an H2X assisted raid on the port of Wilhelmshaven. Radar bombing would be a regular feature as poor weather conditions recurred with the onset of winter. The poor weather led to reduced enemy fighter activity as well. Coastal targets were chosen for early H2X raids because the geography gave good returns on the still-unreliable radar scopes. The crews were also heartened to have escort from the newly arrived P-38s although the Luftwaffe was to have the better of the battle during the initial encounters with Lockheed's twin-tailed aircraft. The largest 381st BG formation was flown to Bremen, where the twenty-seven bombers added their loads of 500 pound GP and 100 pound incendiaries to the general devastation. Gelsenkirchen in the Ruhr was next on 5 November but, although fight-

ers were absent, accurate target flak so damaged 42-30852 (LT Hopp) that *BLOWIN' BESSIE* was abandoned off the Dutch coast and the B-17's remains were found during post-War draining operations in the Zuider Zee. LT Butler's B-17 was so badly hit that six crewmen jumped but their action was early, as the pilots regained control and brought their aircraft home. A seventh had a miraculous escape from death. Having removed his oxygen mask prior to jumping LT Brown lost consciousness and accidentally pulled his parachute ripcord. The canopy deployed out through the open nose hatch then wrapped round the ball turret and the force proceeded to pull Brown partially out of the B-17, which was then around 28,000 feet. Pressure sucked off one boot, but despite an outside air temperature of -40 degrees C Brown suffered minimal frostbite; more amazingly where lack of oxygen rendered a man unconscious in two and dead in twenty minutes, Brown survived at least one or two hours at this normally lethal altitude before the formation descended to a normal breathing level.

Wesel's marshaling yards felt the weight of nineteen bomb loads on 7 November, but the main adversary this day was the appalling temperature levels which particularly affected waist gunners at their open positions and six serious frostbite cases were reported. A return to Wesel two days later was thwarted by clouds rising to 29,000 feet and two days later, similar weather conditions caused yet another run to Wesel to be

Group B-17s fly a practice mission over the North Sea during September of 1943. The majority of the B-17Fs in this formation were probably lost during Black Week which culminated in Black Thursday's run to Schweinfurt (14 October). This mission claimed sixty of the 148 bombers lost during Black Week.

Climbing out over a fleecy undercast is the fourth B-17G Flying Fortress to arrive at Ridgewel. Early B-17Gs did not carry cheek gun mountings, only the Bendix chin turret. This Fortress survived many months of hard combat and moved to AFSC on 19 May 1944.

"aborted." What was a wearying trip to Knaben's molybdenum mines in Norway was a happy occasion for CAPT Baltrusaitusle's 532nd BS crew for they had completed the 'Magic 25" and were free to return to the States. SGT McGaughey nearly did not join his crew in their celebrations — the back-plate on his ball turret fell off and the next few minutes were hectic as he strove to hold his precarious position.

Only one more completed mission was made in November, to Bremen - another target of fearful reputation in the eyes of the 381st BG. On this occasion the only injuries were caused by anoxia, frostbite and burns from electrically heated suit malfunctions. Bremen would feature prominently in the final missions for 1943.

December started badly with four losses over Leverkusen in the Ruhr. LT Hess flying *BACTA T'SAC* (42-3540, the first B-17G received) lost his No 3 engine before the IP and rapidly lost contact. No 2 engine was taken out by a Bf 110's fire and bombs were jettisoned. The crew were hardly encouraged by the appearance of a P-47 going down in flames and narrowly missing their B-17 as it fell. Fatal damage was then inflicted by two Bf 109s and all ten crewmen jumped. SGT Macklin subsequently had a foot amputated from wounds received and SGT Delp died from his wounds. Flight Officer Noxon's veteran crew, just back from the rest-home (nick-named "the flak house") went down with *FOUR ACES/PAT HAND* (42-31111) and a third 535th BS crew led by F/O Sunde was missing in 42-31097. The 532nd BS provided the other loss when LT Jason Duncan in *FULL BOOST* (42-29506) was shot down. A fifth B-17 staggered back to a heavy crash-landing in Kent which caused serious injuries to three officers.

This old farmhouse, within the airfield boundary and close by the control tower, served as the 535th BS Operations Headquarters building.

Four days later a mission to Paris was uneventful for the Group but significant to the future progress of the daylight offensive. The unfamiliar shape of an American fighter looking rather like the Bf 109 in outline appeared off the flanks of the bomber stream. The North American P-51B Mustang was at last in operational service and the promise of full and effective fighter cover for the beleaguered bombers would soon be fulfilled.

North German ports occupied the 8th's attention in mid-December with Emden (11th) and then three Bremen strikes (11th, 16th and 20th). It was on the last of these Bremen runs that fortune again deserted the 381st BG. Thirty B-17s were reaching for the target at 1147 when the Luftwaffe made a slashing strike from behind. The Low Squadron and its second element in particular bore the brunt. LT Crossan in *THE REBEL* (42-31075) was disabled and fell out but managed to bomb before disappearing into the thick contrails exuded by the formation. Only seven men survived as the B-17 came down near Wesermunde. No 3 in the second element was TINKERTOY and her end was tragically fitting for an aircraft with a "jinxed" reputation because an encroaching Bf 109 struck her tail section. The veteran B-17 momentarily stayed under control then flipped into a spin and exploded a few hundred feet into its terminal descent. LTs Lane and Johnson (pilots) and two others scrambled clear before *TINKERTOY* disintegrated. LT Bernard Hollenkamp's 42-3563 was the third B-17 to be culled from the Group's ranks and the fourth was that other veteran *WHALETAIL II*. Her loss

LT Frank Chapman (center) was a 535th BS "original" pilot who became Squadron Ccommanding Officer after MAJ Ingenhutt was shot down on 8 October 1943. Radio/Operator Gunner Ed Myers (fourth from left) was the Group's first evader, being shot down on 3 September and regaining England in late October. Copilot Melvin Hecker (left) completed his tour in the Spring of 1944.

The solid undercast beneath THIS IS IT was a major hindrance to accurate bombing. This B-17 came from 305th BG in August where it had served since February. It was finally transferred out to the SAD (Strategic Air Depot) in May of 1944.

Original ground officers and line chiefs of the 534th BS. The officer to right is LT Paul Stull, killed in a local flight in MIS ABORTION/STUFF on 3I Mar 1944. Second left (standing) is TSGT Percy Casey who was transferred to a B-29 Group heading for the Pacific in 1944.

No Allied fighter such as this Spitfire Mk V would fly so close to a bomber formation unless it was a training mission since bomber gunners fired first and asked questions afterwards. Additionally, fighters positioned this close in could do little to keep the Luftwaffe at arms length from the "Big Friends".

was particularly tragic; flak tore away almost all of the left stabilizer causing the B-17 to become almost unmanageable even with full normal power. LT Leo Canelake limped out over the North Sea, still holding formation. Hopes were improving for *WHALETAIL*'s survival as the English coast neared but about seventy miles from relative safety the B-17 was spotted low down and making a 180 degree turn . Final impact with the frigid water was unobserved and the dark maw of the North Sea had swallowed up another ten souls without a trace. *WHALETAIL II* and *TINKERTOY* had come into existence together and survived many months of fierce combat together. The initial first six months of combat were signaled on 22 December by a strike against Osnabruck. Unbeknown to the crews, time for a change in overall command was fast approaching. COLNazzaro having been marked down for further promotion.

Christmas Eve saw no respite from combat, although the target was just across the Channel at Cocove where V-1 sites were plastered by twenty-eight B-17s. So the fifth Christmas Day of the Second World War arrived with the Allied countries in a mood of sober confidence. Now the feeling was not whether the war could be won but, rather when the enemy would finally be vanquished.

Weather conditions now intervened to cancel operations until 30 December when the first of two consecutive long-range missions were launched. Ludwigshafen's oil refineries were bombed, using H2X due to cloud cover (oil would prove to be the true "Achilles Heel" of the German industrial effort, but was not given priority until mid-1944). This was the last mission for COL Nazzaro and SGT Hickman but with tragically different outcomes. The latter was found slumped at his post and dead due to anoxia (lack of oxygen); ice in his oxygen mask had probably blocked the air-flow but his mask hose was also disconnected.

'OLE FLAK SACK' rests on her belly on the runway at Ridgewell. Wires have been attached to drag her clear of the runway. All but two of LT Arthur Sample's crew were Killed In Action (KIA) in this bomber when it was one of the seven lost over Bremen on 8 October 1943.

(Right) CAPT Dexter Lishon (2nd left kneeling) and his crew pose with their aircraft just twenty-four hours before they abandoned their B-17F BOBBY T (42-30722) on 8 October 1943. The crew were an "original" element of the 534th Bomb Squadron.

Smiling WAC admires the Distinguished Service cross awarded LT Thomas A. Sellars on 18 December 1943. Ceremony was held at Eighth Bomber Command Headquarters at High Wycombe. Sellers received the DSC for his actions in bringing TINKERTOY home after the pilot was killed.

This apparatus was specially constructed by 535th BS ground crewmen to help them change aircraft tires safely. Improper removal of tires under high pressure could and did cause injury or death whenever a tire blew-out.

The horrors of aerial combat are illustrated by the holes in *TINKER-TOY*'s cockpit frame marking the entry point of the cannon shells that decapitated LT Hal Minerich, the pilot. LT Thomas Sellars (copilot) flew the bomber home despite being wounded. Spraying blood froze on the top turret base prevented SGT Miller from manning the position.

Tragic aircraft, tragic crew. *TINKERTOY* had a jinxed reputation and was finally lost on 20 Dec 1943 in a collision with a Bf 109 fighter LT Harold Henslin (left front) was nearing the end of his'tour when he was Killed In Action (KIA) on 28 April 1944.

LT Sellars and the surviving crew stand by *TINKERTOY*'s shattered nose. Despite the scale of damage, neither man in the nose compartment was wounded. LT Sellars later received America's second highest award, the Distinguished Service Cross. Only one other man from the Group was to be so honoured during Group's twenty-two month combat tour.

18

MICKY FINN, a B-17F Flying Fortress of the 534th BS flies over scattered cloud during late1943. MICKY FINN was written off after crash-landing on 4 February 1944 with LT J. Kuhl in charge.

(Right) The nose art on FOUR ACES/PAT HAND was carried under the cockpit on the port side of the aircraft only. The aircraft was lost on 1 December 1943.

The painted-out codes on this 532nd BS B-17F (PU) indicate it previously served with the 303rd BG (Molesworth). The aircraft survived the hard Winter of 43/44 and was finally transferred to AFSC on 4 May 1944.

1 December 1943 was a bad day with four bombers declared Missing In Action. One of these was the FOUR ACES/PAT HAND of the 535th Bomb Squadron which is the rear aircraft in this line-up on the perimeter track at Ridgewell.

The third B-17F lost on 1 December 1943, was FULL BOOST of the 532nd Bomb Squadron flown by LT Jason Duncan. The Fortress was formerly with the 305th BG and was named YE WHITE SWAN when based at Chelveston.

SUGAR of the 534th Bomb Squadron suffered a right landing gear collapse and was transported to the repair depot on a mobile support frame. The Fortress left the 381st Bomb Group in May of 1944.

B-17Fs of the 381st BG fly over extremely inhospitable Norweigan mountains around the Knaben molybdenum mines on 16 November 1943. This Fortress, Winsome Winn Hilda of the 534th Bomb Squadron, was lost on 7 January 1944.

Over-sized code letters are carried on this B-17F named LUCKY STRIKE. The Fortress originally came from the 305th BG in September of 1943 and was written off after a crash-landing at Cawston on 4 January 1944; two of LT Evans crew were killed in the incident.

Much needed gunnery practice at the gun butts. Gunners claims were always much higher than actual confirmed 'kill' figures -- hardly surprising when to fire a heavy gun like the Browning .50 caliber from a swaying bomber required accuracy of sighting and deflection almost impossible to achieve in such pressurized circumstances.

1944

Effective 1 January 1944, COL Nazzaro handed over command to LCOL Harry P. Leber Jr. In fact, COL Joe, as he was respectfully known, had already departed on 31 December, having been given no time to say his farewells prior to reporting to Bomber Command Headquarters. He left behind an organization well seasoned in combat, but inevitably different from the one he had brought over to England. In fifty-four missions most of the original forty crews and aircraft were sad Missing In Action statistics, but this basic fact of aerial combat had to be acknowledged and not dwelt upon.

One of the worst imaginable fates for combat crews was to fall on the last mission. On 4 January, LT Cecil Clore cracked open the throttles on 42-31278 and thundered down the runway bound for Kiel. Shortly afterwards he was heard to say he had problems and was returning. A desperate attempt to crash-land in a field almost came off, but one wing probably struck a group of trees and the resultant impact detonated the bomb-load. Instead of a safe passage to the States, LT Clore found permanent interment at the American Military Cemetery Cambridge along with the other nine men in his crew. The remaining crews successfully bombed Kiel under a P-38 escort cover, but on return *LUCKY STRIKE* (42-29923) reached her end when LT Evans made a heavy crash-landing at Cawston in which two men were killed. The 8th was stretching out into Central Europe once again even without adequate fighter cover as January's experience was to prove. Paraday/Meslay airfield near Tours,

CLUGALUG put in a fair number of missions according to the scoreboard.on her nose She was destroyed when she hit trees during a slow time test on 29 December 1943. The aircraft was struck off the group inventory after the accident.

WHALETAIL's replacement in 534th BS was *WHALETAIL II*, although both were "original" 381st Bomb Group B-17s. *WHALETAIL II* was a Vega-built aircraft and came off the production line just ahead of *TINKERTOY*. Both were lost on 20 December 1943 over Bermen.

France received an accurate pounding but a price was paid, when LT Zeman's 42-30676 was hit by a rocket in the bomb-bay while bombing. A slow turn to the right was reversed and then the B-17 went into a spin from which only some of the crew escaped, one clearing the aircraft below 900 feet altitude. In the remaining five January missions, only one was free of loss (St. Adrian on the 21st). What was another long run to Ludwigshafen on the 7th, proved comfortable for all but *WINSOME WINN HILDA* (42-3078). The regular mount for LT Arden Wilson was disabled in the No 1 engine and limped home with the formation for a time before becoming detached. Enemy fighters engaged the B-17F, one of the relatively few now in Group service, and although two of the attackers were knocked down they shot down *WINSOME WINN HILDA* which crashed with two dead crewmen, the other eight getting out. Ironically, a fellow 534th BS pilot (LT John Silvernale) had noticed Wilson very carefully checking his escape equipment before takeoff! Although his efforts were in vain, Wilson did survive as a POW.

It was now almost three months since regular strikes into Central Europe had been made but the main principle of Operation POINT-BLANK still had to be fulfilled, namely breaking the Luftwaffe by bombing aircraft production plants as well as bringing its pilots up into combat, where American fighters could destroy them. Escort strength was still dangerously thin but nevertheless on 11 January the new boss of the 8th, GEN Jimmy Doolittle ordered his subordinates to carry out a strike at aircraft assembly plants at Oschersleben and Halberstadt less than 100 miles SW of Berlin and "deep in there." The former target was assigned the 1st Division, with the lst CBW leading. Another day of torment lay ahead, mainly for the 533rd BS. In steadily deteriorating weather conditions, the bombers headed out. Recall signals were ultimately sent from HQ but since the lst D was judged to be well into Europe such signals were only despatched to the 2nd and 3rd Divisions. The lst AD force numbered less than 200 bombers and was further split between the two targets. To add to its problems the promised fighter cover was largely absent through a mixture of weather and failure to properly rendezvous with the bombers. Consequently, the Luftwaffe attacks which commenced just inside the Dutch/German border were largely free from interference. LT Nason's novice crew already had problems at this point and Nason turned for home. Their homeward path crossed the waters of the Zuider Zee when the bale out order was given. Five men including SGT John Lantz jumped and seconds later Lantz recalled the B-17 exploding. Their good fortune at having escaped incineration in the bomber was soon cruelly crushed by drowning or exposure to the freezing Dutch waters. Lantz was the sole sur-

Luciky Strike carried a likeness of the famous cigerette brand on the nose along with its mission scoreboard.

vivor and even he was at the point of total exhaustion when a small Dutch vessel's crew fished him out. LT Saur's 42-37962 lost part of its tail to cannon fire causing it to fall into a spin and then break in two; only the two waist gunners scrambled clear while centrifugal force held the others in place until the final impact. At around 1130, as the force neared Osnabruck, LT Matthew McEvoy's 42-29999 *Fertile Myrtle* was observed with a smoking No 4 engine and a short time later it went into a spin. No parachutes were seen but happily the crew did escape. Next to go was LT Ernest Klein in 42-31417. His crew had already come through a bad experience over Bremen on a previous mission, but this time they were not coming home. Both inboard engines were afire as the bomber fell out near Hildesheim but nine men bailed out in time, although one was seen by LT Klein lying dead after the pilot reached the ground. Yet another crew from the 533rd BS was cut from the formation, but only the radio/operator gunner, who was killed at his station by cannon shell fire went in with the plunging B-17.

Up in the CBW Lead B-17, all was not well. Structural damage had adversely affected the bomb-sight and the Group's bombs went astray. Heading the 381st BG's bombing effort was a regular lead bombardier, CAPT Darrell Debolt. Lead Bombardier work was an acquired art and Debolt was a sound exponent of that art. His sighting was superb and the Group's bombs went "right on the button" with the following Groups adding to the punishment. The overall strike left the Focke Wulf production plant badly damaged. The tired bomber crews were more concerned with survival as they turned for home, but the 381st BG's tribulations were not over. Three more B-17s, 42-5878 (LT Perot) 42-3514 (LT Chason) and 42-3118 *GREEN HORNET* (LT Larsen), went down before the enemy coast was cleared. At debriefing there were loud complaints about the indifferent navigation by the CBW Lead Navigator which was reckoned to have taken the formations over some of the worst flak areas. To add to the general sense of gloom the Group was diverted to the 44th BG's base near Norwich from where the crews were transported by road to Ridgewell. A total of forty-two B-17s were missing from the twin lst BD forces and eighteen were lost from the other two Divisions. These were Schweinfurt levels of casualties which boded ill for the immediate future. Of the eight bombers lost by the Group, six were from the 533rd BS with one each from the 532nd BS and 534th BS. This was the mission for which the entire participating lst Division Groups were awarded a DUC which was Ridgewell's second.

It was to be another ten days before the 8th again fulfilled a mission in strength with yet another tilt at V-1 sites in the Pas de Calais. The slight enemy opposition allowed units to make numerous bomb-runs, although the 535th BS brought their ordnance home.

Heading for Frankfurt on 24 January the enemy coast was minutes behind the out-bound 381st BG when the recall signal was received. What depressed crews was the absence of "sortie credit." reaching this stage of a mission for no gain was truly stressful for most crewmen. Another five day gap with two 'scrubbed' briefings ended with a completed run to Frankfurt where heavy flak caused damage to a number of bombers, although fighter attacks were slight. Nevertheless two 534th BS crews (LT Mohnacky in 42-38045 and LT Mickow flying 42-37884) failed to return. The final month's mission was to Brunswick next day. Among the six 535th BS B-17s taking part was the venerable *CHAPS FLYING CIRCUS* (42-30029), Its original pilot, CAPT Frank Chapman, had finished his tour as the commander of the 535th BS along with most of his crew but "his" B-17 would not be so fortunate. LT Carl Baur took her out to Brunswick where visual bombing was rendered impossible by heavy cloud. As the formation was crossing out, Baur called saying he was going to ditch. He sounded cheerful over the intercom and the sea conditions appeared to be smooth enough for a successful water landing. The Group's offer to the Air Sea Rescue to send some aircraft to assist was turned down on the grounds that all was well in hand. When next day it was announced that the B-17F was missing

the Ridgewell personnel felt both distressed and resentful. Only LT Baur's body was recovered on the English coast and the other men were never found.

B-17F *MARTHA II* (42-29761) had arrived from the 96th BG in mid-July but the Brunswick mission was her last as it was with LT Steele's crew, Also lost on his mission was *WOLVERINE* (42-31047) with LT Deering. Deering was the lone warrior who had missed Group assembly on 13 November and gone well into Europe on his own before realizing his error. This time his luck ran out.

Big Week

The Group only participated in five missions for the main part of February but the deceptively slow pace of operations would accelerate dramatically in the final nine days with Big Week. On the 6th what was hitherto an uneventful mission for LT Henry Putek's crew in 42-0025 heading to Nancy/Essay airfield which took a dramatic turn when an explosion blew out the cockpit windows and filled the flight deck with smoke and flames. TSGT Lifford French was badly burned in a successful attempt to extinguish the fire after which he assisted Putek, the sole officer left on board, to handle the crippled B-17. Three Bf l09s now attacked, fortunately not from head-on, where no firepower was available, and the gunners drove them off. A tortious flight home at

LUCKY STRIKE's shattered fuselage was inspected by British servicemen after it crash-landed at Cawston on 4 January 1944.

4,000 feet was made, through various flak zones including Paris, while Putek and French had to wear their masks against the freezing effects of the slipstream whipping into the blown out windscreen. Even the final landfall near Bournemouth was hazardous since "friendly" flak was encountered and the Radio/Operator Gunner could not inform the ground gunners they were not hostile because the radio was shot out and

FRENCHY's FOLLY undergoing a major repair to her right wing in the group maintenance hangar. Most maintenance was carried out in the open, where the hapless ground crewmen had to endure the extreme damp of East Anglia as well as the usual rain, frost and snow of the British winter.

LT Cecil Clore (532th BS) and several of his crew were on what would have been their final mission on the morning of 4 January when they crashed while attempting a desperate forced-landing shortly after takeoff for Kiel. There were no survivors from the tangled wreckage.

the bomb-doors were jammed in the open position, which probably convinced the British gunners that the bomber was hostile. Fortunately, Putek managed to land after a second attempt at the small nearby airfield. Apart from the loss of one eye (SGT Burgasser) and French's burns, all the other crewmen were uninjured. French's gallantry was later recognized by the second award to a 381st BG member of the DSC.

The 6th mission was the fourth in successive days with Wilhemshaven/Frankfurt and St. Avord attacked. The second of these missions caused more adverse comment on the navigational ability of the CBW lead aircraft — naturally the unit in question was once again the 91st BG. Trailing the formation that day was LT John Kuhl in *MICKY FINN* (42-30834), with both right side engines out. He got back to only to discover the starboard landing gear was jammed and the port would only partially deploy. Despite this he made a good landing alongside the runway — the second time for Kuhl who had bellied-in WHODAT on 20 December

One more run to Ludwigshafen (11th) triggered off an eight day spell without activity. The sole loss on the 11th was LT Laux in 42-31099. Up to now, aircraft names were added by combat or ground crews. London having been heavily 'blitzed, it was decided to name four B-17s after London districts most heavily hit. *BERMONDSAY BATTLER*, *LONDON AVENGER* and *ROTHERHITHEIS REVENGE* were names assigned to 381st BG aircraft and Councillor Gibson, chairman of the War Loans Committee christened the latter at a ceremony on the 15th. Only "Revenge" was a new B-17 in combat terms and a complete log of *BERMONDSAY BATTLER* was kept. She was already a nine mission veteran and her regular pilot was LT Lee W. Smith (535th BS).

This B-17F was an "original" of the 533rd BS . The Fortress was destroyed in a bomb loading accident on 23 June 1943.

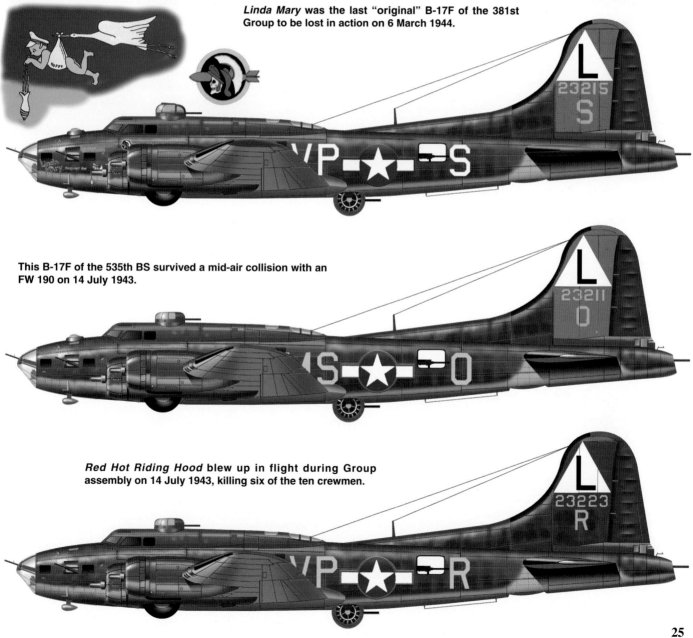

Linda Mary was the last "original" B-17F of the 381st Group to be lost in action on 6 March 1944.

This B-17F of the 535th BS survived a mid-air collision with an FW 190 on 14 July 1943.

Red Hot Riding Hood blew up in flight during Group assembly on 14 July 1943, killing six of the ten crewmen.

Oschersleben on 11 January 1944 was another day of heavy losses for the 381st Bomb Group, with six of the eight losses suffered by the 533rd Bomb Squadron. One of these was *FERTILE MYRTLE* flown by LT Matthew McEvoy. All of the crew baled out successfully.

WINSOME WINN HILDA of the 534th BS is about to go into the Missing In Action category. The No 1 engine was disabled and the bomber was finally downed by enemy fighters, but not before a running fight in which at least two FW 190s were credited to LT Arden Wilson's gunners. The target was Ludwigshafen and the mission was flown on 7 January 1944.

The ultimate fate of these aircraft would reflect the extremes of combat fortunes in the months to come.

The destruction of the Luftwaffe was very much top priority at "Pinetree" and GENs Spaatz and Doolittle set plans in motion for a sustained campaign of attrition aimed at aircraft plants. Since most lay out-

side immediate escort cover, bomber losses of up to twenty percent were allowed for. Weather conditions of low cloud prevailed on Sunday, 20 February, when 1,003 bombers supported by 835 fighters rose to do battle by attacking five plants in the Leipzig/Bernberg/Oschersleben complex. Ridgewell's impressive contribution of forty-one aircraft was split between Leipzig (24) and Oschersleben (17). Good visual bombing at both targets was reported. Enemy fighters were largely kept at bay by the escort but a Bf 110 did land fatal strikes on 42-3562 (LT Cogswell). His copilot recollected this happened when his formation element failed to turn promptly with the Group at the IP and were isolated. LT Bill Borrego remembers the shell hits sounding like a thousand sticks beating on a tin roof. Flak shot out Nos 1 and 2 engines and damaged the controls. Fire was coming close to the auxiliary fuel tank in the bomb-bay. With the bombs still in the bomb-bay, the bailout order was given to which eight men responded. Bill's subsequent experience was perhaps typical of shot down crewmen. Landing in a snow drift after a slow descent in freezing conditions, he found a civilian and a servicemen rushing at him from either side, the former won and administered a pistol-whipping to the airman before being persuaded to stop. Forced to carry his parachute, he was taken to three locations within twenty-four hours and then, relieved of his personal effects, was transferred to the Interrogation Center at Frankfurt. Here he was photographed and allotted a room barely able to house a bed. One cup of ersatz coffee and two

A line-up of Group aircraft at Hardwick (44th BG) to where 381st Bomb Group diverted after the disastrous Oschersleben raid. The aircraft on the right is an H2X radar equipped pathfinder ship of the 305th BG. The other B-17 is LT Miller's *OUR MOM* of the 534th BS.

Another feature of early B-17Gs was the retention of open waist windows as seen on *WOLVERINE* of the 535th BS. LT Deeming failed to bring her home on 30 January 1944.

helpings of equally watery turnip soup were the total daily ration. Interrogation followed the same pattern of refusal to answer questions being met by hints that his fate would not be reported back until he was more co-operaive, while the initial offer of a cigarette was promptly canceled. Another variation was the appearance of an elderly "Red Cross" representative with a questionnaire requiring the same range of questions to be answered, which Bill naturally gave the same terse response. After four days of this, he was let out to join his fellow crew members and the following evening they were marched to Frankfurt's marshaling yards and loaded aboard wagons designed for "eight horses or forty men." Several days later, they arrived at Stalag Luft I Barth up on the Baltic coast where fifteen months of incarceration was ended by the arrival of Russian troops.

The second mission of Big Week for the Group was Gutersloh but cloud cover over the target and the secondary forced the CBW to strike Achmer airfield, where tight bomb patterns on hangars and repair shops left a wake of destruction. TSGT John Sinclair, who had gained the first combat award on the group's inaugural mission to Antwerp was flying his final mission. As on his first mission he was wounded (in his heels) but returned safely to Ridgewell. Good as the bombing had been on 21 February, airfields were not the primary target for assault and Oschersleben's FW plant was selected for the third mission of the series. It was there that the Group had received losses on 11 January and more was in store for the combat crews as they headed out over the North Sea.

By January of 1944 very few "original" B-17Fs were left at Ridgewell. *CHAPS FLYING CIRCUS* proved lucky for its regular crew, headed by Frank Chapman, but not so lucky for LT Carl Baur's team when he attempted to ditching on 30 January. No one survived the attempt.

These would only number twelve out of the thirty-one that took off because the assembly was largely thwarted by cloud. The small force formed up with fifteen B-17s of the 91st BG and proceeded into Europe. The absence of escorts and the gradually clearing clouds was an ominous combination but ironically the German fighters intercepted the force about an hour inside hostile territory and as the cloud cover once again began thickening. A few P-51s were in the vicinity but they were heavily outnumbered and had to look largely to their own salvation and leave the bombers to face what was later estimated to involve between 200 and 300 fighter attacks over the next two hours. The pattern of attack seemed to be for B-17s to be singled out and downed individually. MAJ Fitzgerald (recently appointed 532nd BS Commander) lost two sets of wing men. First reported down was LT Lee W. Smith in *BERMONDSAY BATTLER* (42-39895) with the inboard engine fired by the first attack. Smith slipped down under the lead B-17, leveling off some 3,000 feet below and shortly after disappearing. Tragically there were no survivors from the final crash near Hiddesen, where the crew were buried. Close to Bielefed, LT Roling's 42-39946 lost the No 3 engine and pulled out of line. On the ground, a 105MM flak battery

Eight days to live! With exception of LT Sherwood (2nd left kneeling) all other men on LT Lee W Smith's crew were Killed In Action on 22 February 1944; Smith was on the extreme left kneeling. *BERMONDSAY BATTLER* was their regular aircraft which shared their sad fate.

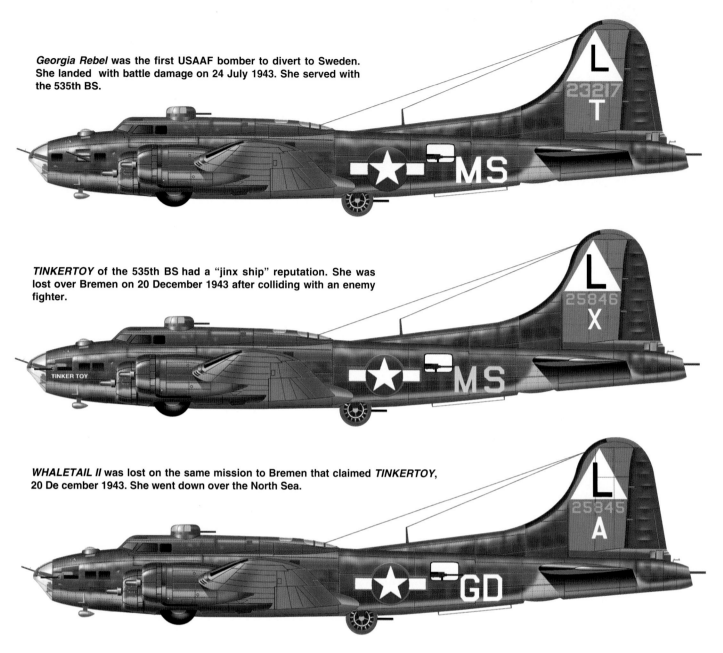

Georgia Rebel was the first USAAF bomber to divert to Sweden. She landed with battle damage on 24 July 1943. She served with the 535th BS.

TINKERTOY of the 535th BS had a "jinx ship" reputation. She was lost over Bremen on 20 December 1943 after colliding with an enemy fighter.

WHALETAIL II was lost on the same mission to Bremen that claimed *TINKERTOY*, 20 December 1943. She went down over the North Sea.

FERTILE MYRTLE was one of six B-17Fs of the 533rd BS to be declared Missing in Action on 11 January 1944 over Oschersleben.

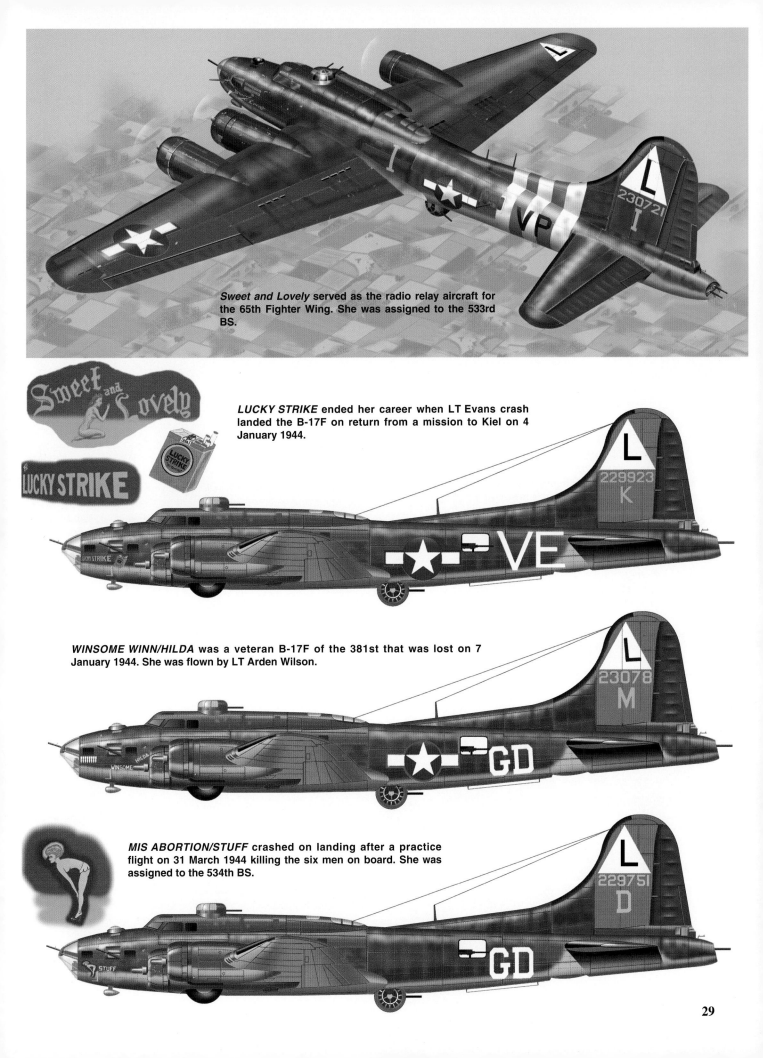

Sweet and Lovely served as the radio relay aircraft for the 65th Fighter Wing. She was assigned to the 533rd BS.

LUCKY STRIKE ended her career when LT Evans crash landed the B-17F on return from a mission to Kiel on 4 January 1944.

WINSOME WINN/HILDA was a veteran B-17F of the 381st that was lost on 7 January 1944. She was flown by LT Arden Wilson.

MIS ABORTION/STUFF crashed on landing after a practice flight on 31 March 1944 killing the six men on board. She was assigned to the 534th BS.

ROTHERHITHE's REVENGE **was christened at the same time as** *BERMONDSAY BATTLER* **but in stark contrast went on to complete around 120 missions.** *REVENGE* **has hit a soft patch in the runway and embedded her left landing gear in the process.**

sighted on the formation and in the two minutes the B-17s were within range, forty-eight salvoes were fired. Halfway through the barrage, the German observers saw a B-17 (Roling's aircraft) fall into the clouds. It emerged in a terminal dive crashing at Leopoldshohe. The aircraft's nose section had been shot away and the officer complement along with the engineer were killed, leaving the five other crewmen to bale out.

Two more bombers were lost before the target which was not even

Big Week's first mission had no aircraft losses for the Group, but one of the crew was wounded. The extent of his injury was uncertain but the fact that he was being attended to inside the aircraft suggests something serious. The mission was flown on 20 February 1944.

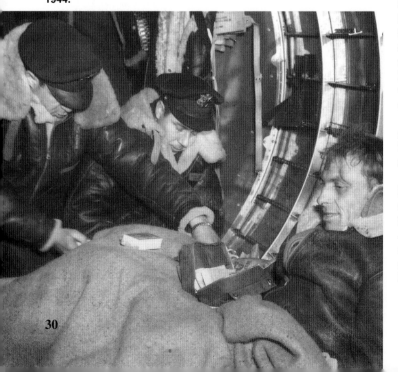

bombed, because it was obscured by cloud. Two more went down while an unspecified location at Bunde, southwest of Minden was bombed. The unlucky quartet were LT Flaherty in 42-31443 (unwisely named *FRIDAY THE 13th*), LT Hustedt with 42-31696 along with his fellow 535th BS crews, LT Downey in 42-31533 and LT Francis Fridgen with 42-97474. The latter attempted a crash-landing from which only two or three men emerged alive, including SGT Lowell Slayton.

The shock of Oschersleben was still new when a briefing to another "hornet's nest" was called — Schweinfurt. MAJ Shackley was in charge for what was his third run as leader. He felt that a knockout blow was landed on this occasion as the plants were smothered in tight bomb patterns. This proved to be optimistic although much damage had been inflicted. Big Week's final strike was the next day (25th) and the Messerschmitt factory at Augsburg was the target . The eleven bombers in the Composite Group achieved a good strike but the twenty B-17s making up the low group were not so fortunate. The leader (LT John Silvernale) suffered a bomb-bay hit on the bomb-run which dislodged the smoke markers and set them on fire. Fearful of his bomb-load being detonated by the fire, Silvernale released and many in the formation took this as their signal to follow suit and all their ordnance fell harmlessly short. One aircraft was missing from the Composite Group; this was 42-37786 flown by LT Don Henderson (532nd BS). The crew was on its final mission, but fighter attacks in the target area knocked the B-17 out to a trailing position. It was last seen over a large forest and probably smashed into the ground a short time later. All the enlisted men, bar the engineer, were killed on board as was the navigator. The four survivors came down by parachute.

The results of Big Week, although impressive, were not decisive largely due to German inventiveness in dispersing their industries. Indeed, overall production levels actually increased almost to the War's end. Pilots were harder to replace; however, and as the increasing numbers of American fighters began to seek out their opponents instead of passively acting as bomber escorts. This policy was encouraged by GEN Doolittle and the steady drain in dead and injured personnel inflicted upon the Luftwaffe was a hemorrhage which would never be stanched.

The American authorities reckoned that if any target would guarantee

FRIDAY THE THIRTEENTH, in the foreground, sadly lived up to her unlucky image on 22 February 1944, when she was lost along with five other 381st Group bombers. The pilot was LT Francis Flaherty. Aircraft at the top is SQUAT N'DROPPIT from the 535th BS

By early 1944, MARTHA II was one of a handful of B-17Fs still in service with the Group, but she was downed on 30 January. The B-17G accompanying her was another Missing In Acaction statistic on 25 February when LT Don Henderson (on his last mission) put her down in enemy territory.

a fierce reaction from the Luftwaffe, it would be Berlin. RAF Bomber Command was already finding this out to its increasing cost as the German night-fighter force was penatrating the cloak of darkness under which its Lancasters and Halifaxes flew during the series of operations in 1943/44 known as "The Battle Of Berlin". Better fortune would attend the 8th's efforts but prior to the March series of Berlin missions, there was natural trepidation of the likely cost entailed in such regular assaults, since Berlin was "way in there."

The initial pair of missions (3 and 4 March) were aborted by bad weather. On the first occasion, there was a mid-air collision between a 94th BG B-17 and another from an unidentified Group. Remnants from the exploding bombers fell on LT Rogers Fortress 42-37986 and sent it out of control. The next day was a repeat cancellation but not before a veteran B-17F (42-30151) with LT Keyes in charge was added to the MIA list (the recall signal was ignored by a small 3rd Division force headed by the 95th BG on 3 March which went on to bomb "Big B" through heavy cloud).

Two days later and "with the queues to the toilets three times as long" according to one crewman present at briefing, the third run to Germany's capital was outlined. This time 672 bombers covered by some 800 escorts would get through. Fighter opposition was constant most of the way in and even over the city. Near Magdeburg, LT Coyle's aircraft was hit hard and peeled off with its right wing enveloped in flames. All but SGT Legg jumped into captivity from LINDA MARY; a

MAJ James G. Brown (Group Chaplain) poses, second from left-front, with LT Wood's crew prior to participating in the first of five (officially unapproved) missions on 2 Mar 1944. Chaplains were "non-combatants" under military law.

bit of Group history attended the aircraft's loss, since she was the last "original" Group bomber to be declared MIA. Two other crews joined the total of sixty-nine bombers and eleven fighters lost. LT Fastrup got all his men out of 42-31448 while LT Haushalter (534th BS) flying 42-31553 lost half his crew. All three losses occurred around the Madgeburg sector.

The 1st CBW was leading the entire 8th Air Force with the 91st BG the CBW leader. As its Lead Bombardier was sighting on the Erkner ball-bearing plant, a ridge of cloud obscured the target. While the 91st BG sought its own "Target of Opportunity", succeeding Groups were advised to do the same. As a result, the 381st BG became the first unit from the initial full-scale Berlin assault to bomb around Zernsdorf, some seven miles SW of the Primary target. The return home was made without further direct loss over the Continent, but LT Cahill in 42-37983 failed to make the English coast and ditched, happily with no fatalities.

Berlin was re-visited on 8 and 9 March with noticeably smaller casualties, especially on the latter day when only nine bombers were missing. One Group loss was suffered on 8 March, LT Pirtle in 42-38029. A full week now elapsed before the 381st BG was called back into action. This time to Augsburg in Southern Germany with COL Leber and MAJ Halsey (535th BS commander) leading thirty-three aircraft. One man finishing his tour on this mission, was LT Thomas Sellars who, as TIN-KERTOY's copilot, had brought her home after the pilot was detapitated, an action that earned him the DSC.

Flying prolonged distances in socked in weather conditions could and did lead to formations going dangerously off-course. This seems to have been the case on 20 March when barely half the force of 230 B-17s got through to Mannheim and then started to stray anything up to 100 miles South of the briefed route. LT George Mackintosh had been the copilot on GEORGIA REBEL when it diverted to Sweden on 24 July 43. He was also a DFC holder, this award arising from his bringing home OUR DESIRE (42-21357) on 21 Feburary with a burnt nose section and gaping bomb doors as well as being short of his navigator and bombardier. Now on his fourteenth mission he was startled to find, that when he broke cloud cover he was over what turned out to be the Normandy coast rather than the briefed cross-out point at the Pas de Calais. Already suffering engine failure on one engine his Fortress, JAYNEE B (42-31381), now suffered similar failures in two of the remaining engines, leaving him with no choice but to ditch just off the coast. Only one dinghy could be inflated into which eight men scrambled, leaving Mackintosh and SGT Eugene Copp (a gunnery instructor on a three-mission detachment from the States) to cling onto the raft-

PRINCESS PAT, a B-17G of the 533rd Bomb Squadron carries a very faded and weathered camouflage. The port outboard wing panel was probably a replacement since it carried the national insignia with a Red surround and the insignia on the fuselage has a Blue surround. The insignia change from Red to Blue took place during September of 1943.

(Left) Marvin Lord of the 532nd Bomb Squadron is outfitted with typical flight gear for a B-17 crewman. He is waring a Mae West life preserver, oxygen mask, parachute harness and helmet with built in earphones.

B-17Gs of the 381st Bomb Group fly a practice mission escorted by a P-51B Mustang. The introduction of the Mustang made escorted missions to Berlin and beyond possible and greatly reduced bomber losses during late 1944 and throughout the rest of the war.

This was the third B-17G to arrive at Rockwell. She was damaged by rockets on 9 October 1943 and lost over Bremen on 20 December 1943.

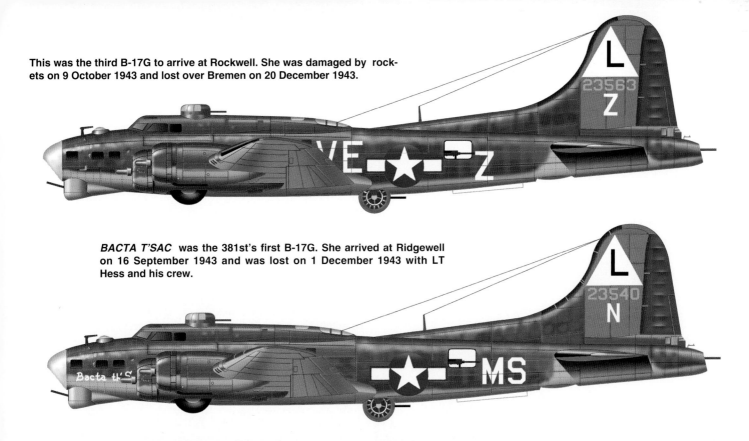

BACTA T'SAC was the 381st's first B-17G. She arrived at Ridgewell on 16 September 1943 and was lost on 1 December 1943 with LT Hess and his crew.

WOLVERINE was an early production B-127G with open waist gun positions. She was lost on 30 January 1944 while being flown by LT Bob Deering.

SCHNOZZLE was lost in a mid-air collision over Ridgewell on 21 January 1944. She was assigned to the 534th BS.

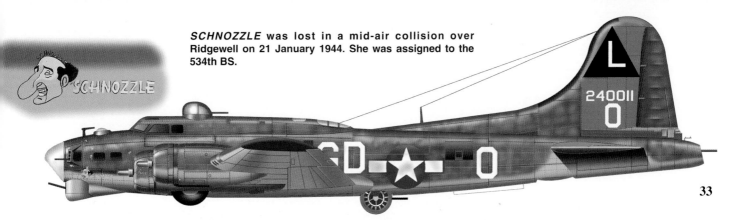

33

LINDA MARY unloads M47 incendiaries in the company of younger B-17Gs. The 533rd BS bomber was the last "original" aircraft to be declared Missing In Action over Berlin on 6 Mar 1944 with LT Richard 'Slick' Coyle at the controls.

In addition to three Group losses on the first full Berlin mission, LT Cahill was forced to slide this 532nd BS aircraft into the sea off Foreness Point. The tail section of the B-17G lies beached on English coastline.

lines. Fortunately, a French boat soon picked them up saving them from the deadly numbing Channel waters to begin the long haul to a POW camp. They survived an RAF attack on Frankfurt while they were passing through the town. In Mackintosh's case, he finished up in Stalag Luft III where, in May, he was re-united with *GEORGIA REBEL*'s pilot Osce V. Jones. LT Beckman flying MALE CALL (42-97471) with CAPT Winters, was coming home from his final mission along with seven of his crew. As he was completing his landing run the main gear collapsed but "any landing you walk away from is a good landing" proved true in this case.

The fourth Berlin mission was on 22 March and a solid undercast all the way was matched by virtually no aerial opposition, although the flak was unhindered and was intense at several points along the route. This mission was the first in a succesive three day spell. On the last, the Group was to experience three losses of the most tragic kind On takeoff the freshman crew of LT Kenneth Haynes had barely cleared

This B-17 of the 534th BS, named *WHODAT*, rides a steady but tor-turously slow path through a concentrated flak barrage during the bomb-run up to the target.

Ridgewell's boundary, before the B-17 (42-38102) stalled and crashed near Birdbrook village. The resultant detonation scattered parts far and wide and left the medical teams nothing to do but salvage what human remains they could find. Conditions of thick clouds and heavy contrails streaming from the formations contributed to two further Group losses. As Frankfurt was approached, the B-17s of LTs Thomson (42-40008) and LT Rickerson (42-31490) collided. Thomson reportedly peeled away, still under control while Rickerson's aircraft split in two. In actual fact,the latter B-17 staggered back as far as Pas de Calais, where it was bellied-in and was set on fire by the crew. Three down without enemy interference was a body blow and must have reinforced the combat crews opinion that the elements were often as great a hazard as the Germans.

March ended with a quartet of daily missions. On the third mission an "impossible" incident occured. Rheims/Champagne airfield had just felt the weight of thirty bomb loads when two shells burst around the tail section of WHODAT (42-37754). The effect was to practically sever the tail, which was left hanging on by mere shards of metal. This hit also killed the waist and tail gunners. With the elevators jammed in the up position and with severed rudder cables, LT Dan C. Henry and LT

Crisler somehow pulled their battered B-17 out of its dive and headed for home with eight P-38s as escort. SGT Quaresma managed to lash enough of the rudder cables together to provide some control for the pilots. Luckiest of the seven surviving crew was SGT Wheatley, whose turret was in the vertical position when *WHODAT* was hit. This was the only angle possible for entry and exit in and out of the ball and since he could not wear a parachute inside the turret, it is clear what his fate would have been had his turret been in any other angle. When Ridgewell was reached the other five crewmen jumped (attempts to land being too risky). Henry and Crisler then took their gallant cripple out over the Essex coast where they jumped leaving *WHODAT* to fall harmlessly into the sea.

LT Liddle's *SUPERSTITIOUS ALOYSIUS* (42-37933) was also heading for her last mission. On the way out, an engine caught fire and Liddle aborted. As altitude was decreased, the fire (fed by the increased oxygen levels) gained intensity. Finally, over Kent, the bail-out order was given and the crew, including SGT Emory Y. Naha, a full-blooded Tewa Indian ,safely exited. LT Joe Scott used initiative when put up at a local hotel; with no U.S. currency on hand, he persuaded the manager to accept his French escape-kit money.

The final month's mission to Brunswick saw all thirty-one B-17s come home but thirteen were forced to disperse to other airfields beccause of bad weather. The last day of March was free of missions but involved another of those incidents which haunted combat crewmen. Four days before, T/SGT Don Karr had completed twenty missions with LT Silvernale and he had sworn never to fly with any other pilot. He was persuaded this day to make up a "scratch" crew for a local flight in *MIS ABORTION/STUFF*. The short flight was terminating when the B-17 was observed to sharply dip and plough into the fields just short of the runway, killing all on board. There were suggestions later that LT Stull a 534th BS engineer might have been at the controls as an unofficial "trainee." Whatever the cause of the crash, SGT Karr was lost in a cruelly needless manner after surviving the worst the enemy could throw at him. He was buried at Madingley Military Cemetery, Cambridge.

WHODAT's tail was twisted to one side by two shell bursts as it cleared the target on 28 March 1944. LTs Henry and Crisler ordered the other five surviving crew members to bail out over ridgewell then baled out themselves over the Essex coastline leaving *WHODAT* to plunge harmlessly into the sea.

A pair of camoflaged B-17Gs of the 535th BS in early February 1944. MS:U (flown by LT Charles Downey) was gone by 22 Febuary, as one of six lost on the Oschersleben raid, while MS:P was Missing In Action over St. Avord airfield on 28 April 1944 (flown by LT Harold Henslin).

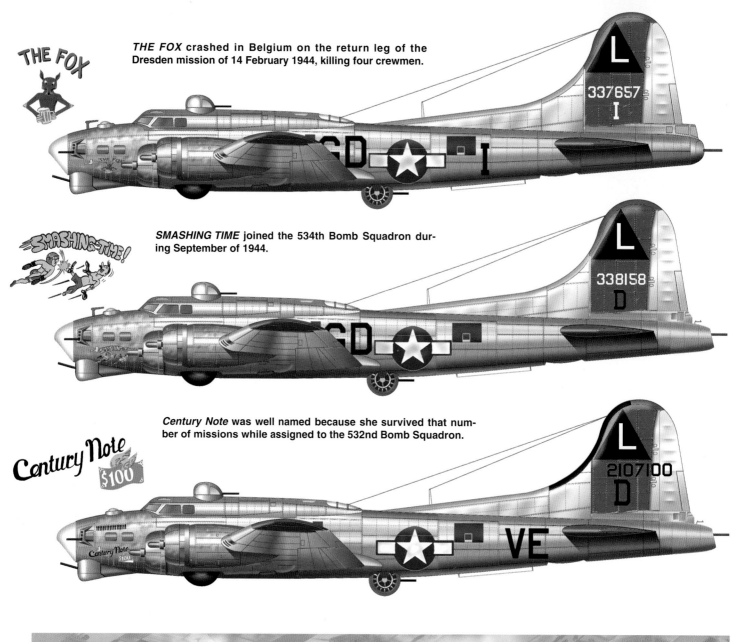

THE FOX crashed in Belgium on the return leg of the Dresden mission of 14 February 1944, killing four crewmen.

SMASHING TIME joined the 534th Bomb Squadron during September of 1944.

Century Note was well named because she survived that number of missions while assigned to the 532nd Bomb Squadron.

PELLA TULIP, of the 532nd BS, was badly damaged by flak over Cologne but made it home with her crew. She was repaired and placed back into service.

These B-17Gs, *FLAK MAGNET* and *SLEEPY TIME GAL* carry full 1st Combat Bomb Wing markings which consisted of Red fin center section, wing tips, and horizontal stabilizers. Both were assigned to the 532nd Bomb Squadron. *FLAK MAGNET* was still on strength with the 381st Bomb Group as of 6 May 1945. *SLEEPY TIME GAL* also had the rudder tirm tab in Red, she was flown by LT David Morgan.

In early 1945, the 8th AF issued orders to remove the ball turrets from selected 381st BG B-17Gs. This Fortress was assigned to the 543th Bomb Squadron and was one of the aircraft involved in the program.

(Above & Below) The name *MIS ABORTION* placed behind the bending female figure on 42-29761 attracted the displeasure of the 8th Air Force high command, but its replacement by the single word *STUFF* went totally unchallenged!

In April of 1944, the Strategic Bomber commands were given over to GEN Eisenhower charge to prepare the way for the upcoming invasion of Europe. Both GEN Spaatz and Air Chief Marshal "Butch" Harris were reluctant to see their forces diverted to tactical bombing; Harris thought his crews were not capable of the degree of bombing accuracy necessary to strike French and Belgian targets without inflicting high civilian casualties, but happily he was to be proved wrong.

Ridgewell records reflect the steady switch between April and June from strategic targets to tactical targets. June was almost totally devoted to the latter with only three strategic targets on the mission tally.

April also recorded the basic victory of the 8th Fighter Command over the Luftwaffe, because from May onwards the Luftwaffe was unable to strike the bomber streams where and when they chose. Instead they would have to resort to slipping in specialized formations of heavily armored fighters and vectoring them onto unprotected elements with the intention of knocking down as many as possible in one fell swoop (the worst noted case being twenty-five out of thirty-seven B-24s of the 445th BG shot down on 25 September 1944).

The first of April's eleven missions went out on the 8th when twenty-nine bombers hit Oldenburg airfield. LT Leslie Bond (534th BS) in his *CAROLINA QUEEN* was faced with a belly-landing on return but was lacking the specialist tools with which to jettison the ball turret to make

MIS ABORTION/STUFF had been at Ridgewell since June of 1943. On 31 March 1944 she was landing off a short local flight when she stalled and nosed into the ground killing LT Wayne Schomberg, LT Stull (534th BS Engineering Officer) and four others.

a smoother impact. LCOL Hall (Air Exec.) took off in a light aircraft with the necessary tools in a sand-ballasted bag which he endeavored to fish in through the B-17's radio hatch. Difficulty in matching speeds forced him to land and go up this time in another B-17 with which a proper transfer was effected. The subsequent crash-landing was pulled off but in the case of the crew it was sadly a case of a temporary reprieve from death or captivity.

Taking off next day in 42-30613 LT Souder (535th BS) made three takeoff attempts of which the last saw his B-17 go off the runway end and pitch onto its nose. Miraculously, although the nose was stove in, there were no serious injuries. The bomber was later "scrapped" while the crew were fated to face the same experience as LT Bond's crew. A short-range run to Brussels (10th) was followed by four missions all of which were long wearying experiences lasting up to eleven hours.

Schweinfurt (on the 13th) claimed LT Mullane in *OUR DESIRE* (42-31357) when the copilot's controls were shot out and other fatal damage inflicted during a second run into the target but all nine men jumped. Similar good fortune attended the loss of *PATCHES N' PRAYERS* (42-27733) with LT Souder in charge over Oranienburg (on the 18th); the returning crews were hardly pleased by having to make a neat formation pass over the airfield for the benefit of GENs Spaatz, Doolittle and Williams — especially the crew bringing home a dead gunner. The next day, a Sunday, the 1st CBW struck at Eschwege and two 381st BG bombers were culled from the Group. LT Rayburn was lost in 42-38004 and LT Leslie Bond in 42-3525. The latter aircraft was hit by a fighter and finally exploded just after LT Mason and SGT Clyman bailed out. They were the sole survivors.

Three of the next four missions were to German locations but ironically it was the sole French target - Metz/Frescaty airfield (25th) which caused the next loss when LT Claytor (535BS) went down in 42-3511. This was the second in a succession of seven daily missions of which the fourth was a cause for particular celebration. The run to Cherbourg was the hundredth completed mission. This milestone had taken ten months and five days to achieve and 178 actual briefings ; the latter figure reflecting the uncertain weather conditions over Europe which regularly

The B-17 in the center is *OUR DESIRE* (42-31357) which was lost on the Group's fourth mission to Schweinfurt on 13 April 1944. LT James Mullane and his crew were captured and spent the rest of the war as POWs.

This 535BS B-17F (42-30613) ran out of runway and nosed over on 9 April 1944. There were no recorded injuries among LT Souder's crew but their lease on freedom lasted a bare nine days, when they went down in *PATCHES N' PRAYERS* (42-37733) over Oranienburg.

forced mission cancellation. The coming months would witness an acceleration in mission-rates for the 8th and the 381st BG was to take barely six months to reach its next "century".

The first 100 missions had climaxed a period in which the Group had endured the Summer of 1943 battles and the 8th's autumn crisis which culminated in Black Week which virtually stalled the daylight offensive until adequate fighter escort was available. Most of the "original" crews and all of the "original" B-17s were gone, but the replacement personnel headed by veterans such as COL Hall and MAJ Shackley were to serve the Group equally well up to D-Day and beyond.

Mission 101 brought home the saying, "there are no easy missions", once again to the crews. St. Avord airfield in France was the lightly defended target which had just been bombed. In the lead was MAJ Osce V. Jones and LT Harold Henslin in *GEORGIA REBEL II* (42-38061). One of the waist gunners, SGT Bill Blackmon, now sighted the first of what appeared to be a tracking series of flak bursts coming from behind. His count never reached four because that burst impacted on the B-17's No 2 engine and tore it off. Bill was thrown to the floor and fought des-

SLEEPY TIME GAL of the 532nd BS was flown by LT David Morgan.

H*APPY BOTTOM* of the 532nd BS was christened by film star Edward G. Robinson. The aircraft was named in honor of his wife, Gladys.

SUGAR was assigned to the 534th Bomb Squadron. She was one of the first B-17Gs delivered to the Group.

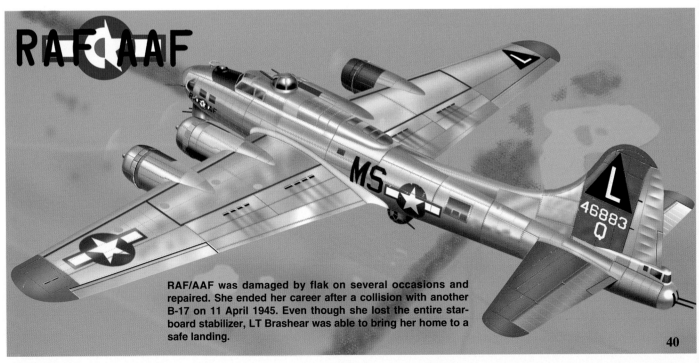

RAF/AAF was damaged by flak on several occasions and repaired. She ended her career after a collision with another B-17 on 11 April 1945. Even though she lost the entire starboard stabilizer, LT Brashear was able to bring her home to a safe landing.

LT Rickerson's bomber, which collided near Frankfurt with another B-17 (42-40008, flown by LT Thomson) on 24 March 1944, staggered back to a make a crash landing in northeast France. The crews and both aircraft were from the 532nd BS.

CAPT Alan F Tucker, a 534th Bomb Squadron "original" pilot, signs in off his last mission sometime in early 1944. He was watched by SGT Raglan.

perately to clear the rear hatch as the bomber went through what felt like a progression of dips and leveling gyrations. In fact, the aircraft had broken into several sections according to SGT Tom O'Brien, a ball turret gunner on another 535th BS B-17 who later reported that he could not imagine any one escaping from the tumbling wreckage. In fact, Bill

Another happy trio from the 535th BS talk animatedly during a Spring 1944 debriefing. Navigator LT Vernon Nicholson (left) has one mission to go while the pilot, LT Bill Ridley is well through his tour. The happiest man is TSGT Lester (center) who just completed his twenty-five missions.

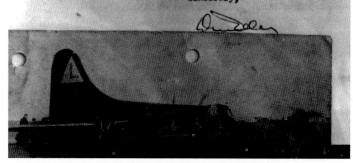

USAFE Box 7306
APO, N.Y., 09012
26 February 1979

U. S. Air Force Museum
Wright-Patterson AFB, Ohio

Gentlemen:

While on a recent trip to France, I had met a Frenchman who had given me the enclosed "picture post card" and asked that I send it to an USAF organization who may want to send copies to any of the crew, who survied the crash landing, and may still be alive.

The photo was taken clandestinely by a local photographer (note the German guards inspecting the tail gun section) and then hawked the souvenir post cards. The back of the card states "Photo of an American Fortress, shot down at CARNIN (Pas-de-Calais /France/. The occupants were safe and sound. April 1944. Souvenir of the 1939-1944 war. Mr. D'Azevedo, Martial, no. 4 rue de Vendore, Courrieur (Pas-de-Calais)" and signature of Mr. D'Azevedo, who had given me the card.

Sincerely,

41

Ridgewell, sometime in 1944, reveals several Group Fortresses taxying along the two short runways. The control tower is to the left of the trees in the upper right. The base had two T2 Type hangars.

Blackmon, SGT Padgett and MAJ Jones did bail out safely. Henslin was not as lucky as was LT Guertin, who, the previous July had accompanied Jones to Sweden in the original *GEORGIA REBEL.*

For the past few months after the 351st BG's transfer to 92nd CBW, the 1st CBW's third Group had been a composite formed from the 381st BG and 91st BG, an arrangement which had not worked too well, at least as far as Ridgewell was concerned. Now with the arrival of the 398th BG at Nuthampstead, the CBW was back to full strength. This "freshman" Group's introduction to combat was unhappy due to a series

of operational planning errors which saw the Group assembly go wrong. Better results attended the next day's mission , which was just as well, since the target was Berlin.

Nineteen full missions, the highest monthly total to date, were to be flown in May with the majority still reflecting the strategic nature of the daylight offensive. Despite this, the first eight were flown without loss, which was gratifying in that the targets were such well defended targets as Berlin Lutzkendorf and Stettin/Stralsund. Then came a mission to Berlin (19th) that spoiled the pattern and reminded the crews of the hard

CAPT Douglas Winters was flying this 532nd BS B-17G along with three other airmen on a local flight when a fire in two engines caused a hasty but successful crash-landing in a field near Halstead, Essex.

facts of combat life. Flak over the Primary (railroad yards) took out LT Blog in 42-32088 and LT Sharp in 42-97454. The former was set on fire in the No 2 engine, dropped out under control and successfully had his crew bail out a few minutes later; all were captured but Blog and LT Dennis were free for forty-eight hours. LT Sharp was watching Blog, when his B-17 was hit in the No 2 engine. The propeller could not be feathered due to oil pressure drop. The loss of Nos 3 and 4 superchargers added to his problems and he lowered his wheels as a signal that he was quitting the formation. His intention was to run for Sweden but complete electrical failure along with the spread of the fire around the No 2 engine forced him to issue the bail out order. A heavy landing resulted in a extremely painful pelvis fracture which hospitalized him until 1 August after which he was sent to Stalag Luft III. All but one of his crew came through, the exception being LT Hardwick, a first mission replacement for Sharp's navigator. He got out, but his parachute never opened.

The 19th signaled the return of hard times before May was out. Berlin came up on the briefing charts five days later and thirty-nine B-17s led by MAJ Fitzgerald headed out in thick cloud and haze with contrails adding to the discomfort. Enemy opposition was minimal up to completion of the bomb-run but here things fell apart at least for the 534th BS. The squadron elected to make a second run and they were still detached from the main formation when a large group of FW 190s and Bf 109s

SGT Bill Blackmon, standing third from left, was one of three survivors from LT Henslin's crew on 28 April 1944. Henslin (second from left - front) was Killed In Action (KIA) with only a handful of missions left on his tour.

(Above & Below) SQUAT N DROPPIT was always in trouble. On 21 January 1944 she chopped off the vertical fin on RETURN TICKET (42-39890) of the 535th BS. On 15 April she landed from a practice flight and caught fire. The fire defied all efforts to extinguish it, destroying the bomber.

came in from behind and below. Their fire-storm was mainly focused on the 534th BS although the main formation was also struck. The action was over quickly as only the one pass was made from a frontal position, but the carnage was terrible. LT Wainwright in 42-31698 and LT Wardenoki in 42-97214 were reported to have collided and nearly caused the loss of LT Williams' *JOANNE* (42-97174). The latter flew through the explosion's fireball which burnt off all fabric from the control surfaces and blackened the windscreen. Even with this damage, Williams and LT Lear came home to a perfect landing. LT Dasso lost his starboard wing outboard of the No 1 engine and then the other wing as he rolled to the right. Only a handful of men survived in *RETURN TICKET* (42-39890). LT Ezzell drifted out and down with crewmen observed to jump (seven got out before 42-38010 crashed near Wilmensdorf). The fifth down was probably LT Higgins who was reported to have exploded but not before four crewmen jumped; sadly Higgins and three others were thirty mission veterans from the 15th Air Force based in Italy. Their 535th BS B-17 (42-31878) came down between Melchow and Biesenthal. LT Gardon was the sixth loss. His B-17 was hit heavily in the nose section and right wing with No 3 engine

PATCHES N PRAYERS was a Douglas-built B-17G whose Natural Metal cheek gun window frame stands out from her camoflaged fuselage. The frame fits over the pitot mast.

SHACK RABBIT (42-31197) from the 533th BS was a Boeing production B-17G with no cheek gun mountings. The lengthened nose canopy was a feature on many Boeing and Douglas built B-17Gs.

on fire. SGT O'Neal recalled that the bomber was dived three times after which he baled out. Only Gardon was definitely killed, although LT Sornberger was badly burnt on his face and hands. The 535th BS *ME AND MY GAL* (42-40017) was set ablaze up front but TSGT Vanderzee, extinguished it promptly. Yet another 535th BS B-17 (42-31990) *STAGE DOOR CANTEEN* was lucky to survive a windmilling propeller which forced it out of formation; skirting several flak fields on the way out. LT Bailey's 533th BS crew had to deploy parachutes from the rear hatches to slow the brakeless bomber on landing.

Blissfully unaware of the air battle was LT Zip Zapinski who had earlier aborted, but while coming home had picked up a distress signal from a ditched aircraft and had acted as guide for a vessel in the vicinity and finally landed after eleven hours. This stunning reverse surely dispelled any hopes that the going was going to get easier with the Luftwaffe pinned down by the 8th Fighter Command. Despite all their mounting problems, the Germans would fight to the last. Three days later another B-17 was added to the Missing In Action tally when LT Stuart was lost in 42-107023. May's penultimate mission was to the Junkers plant at Dessau when the group was CBW lead with GEN Gross up front. Enemy fighters were sighted in growing numbers from about forty miles from the target but when the bomb-run was under way, ten Bf 109s

OL' MAN TUCKER displays the revised cheek gun position which became standard on the B-17G.

lunged at the B-17s from in front. Three bombers were taken down, including LTs Monohan and Burton (both 533th BS) flying 42-38188 and 42-102672 respectively and LT Zapinski (532th BS) in 44-6025. The latter crew were on their twenty-first mission in only fifty days - an indication of how quickly crews were now progressing through their tours compared to the six to eight month average during 1943 and early 1944. LT Bob Van Buskirk later recalled how today was the first occasion for him to operate the Bendix chin turret. His summing up was "I didn't get them but they surely got us." With the No 3 gas tank ablaze, the crew was ordered out of the doomed B-17 and all drifted down to imprisonment. For the second time in six days, LT Yates bomber was crippled and a thirty minute fight for survival saw Yates assisted once again by TSGT Vanderzee, this time as acting copilot after LT Klutho had jumped. Allied fighters finally drove off the attacking fighters and the bomber was brought home on half power. The original recommendations for the Silver Star for both men were reduced to DFCs.

D-Day and Beyond

Bomber crews were generally used to early morning awakenings especially during the summer. Consequently, the CQ (Charge of Quarter's) call to "Up and at them" at 0130 on 6 June was not unusual. But what surely woke them was the announcement that they would be bombing the Normandy coast ten minutes ahead of the Allied invasion fleets. Combat crews were issued sidearms while the station defense element was on full alert. The thirty-four bombers taking part in the first of two sorties under CAPT Enos would strike at gun batteries at Vers-Sur-Mer and Courselles-Sur-Mer. But, what should have been a visual experience of the crews' life-time was anti-climaxed by the lowering clouds which prevented any view of the approaching armada and only intermittent sight of the target. A second formation of twelve B-17s under CAPT Armstead did not even bomb its assigned target near Caen.

Operation OVERLORD had been completely concealed from the bomber crews until the day of the invasion. As the Allied armies steadily pushed back the enemy land forces, the average mission time spent over hostile territory would decline while the relative absence of fighter opposition was another welcome sign. On the other hand, the weight of flak would increase in proportion to the shrinking boundaries of Nazi Germany. Targets, particularly in the oil plant category, headed by Merseberg would hold as much apprehension for this later generation of 8th bomber crews as the fighter-defended targets of 1943/44 had held for their predecessors.

French targets were the order for June as the Allied armies strove to expand their foothold in Normandy. Kerlin Bastard airfield was hit on 7 June, but flak crippled LT Martyniak's *OUR CAPTAIN* (42-97258) so badly that she had to be ditched north of the Channel Isles. Happily all

"Magnificent trails of treachery" stream back from a 381st BG formation. They were not magnificent for the crews since they could lead to the pilots becoming disorientated and ending up in collision, with usually fatal results.

the crew survived and after transferring from their dinghies to a motorized lifeboat dropped by an RAF Warwick of No 276 Squadron were then located by an Air Sea Rescue (ASR) launch, but not before failure of their own motor and partial engine failure of the ASR launch caused the latter to limp home with the lifeboat in tow.

A succession of missions to North and Central France soon caused one Squadron diarist to acidly remark, "Soon we will not be able to make sarcastic remarks about what the Liberator boys do for a living, that is, "Milkruns." It was no such easy experience for LT Tarr on 12 June when Nos 1 and 2 engines were lost in quick succession, with No 2's propeller windmilling and finally flying off and smashing against the fuselage, just as the aircraft was landing.

Bordeaux/Merignac airfield held a "jinx" for the 381st BG since, there were losses on each of the three occasions it was attacked. Both June missions (15th and 19th) had cost one B-17, LT Kelly's 42-38009 and LT Doyle's 42-107088 respectively.

The next day the Group faced Hamburg's fearsome flak barrage which claimed one victim, LT Dunkel's 43-37612. It suffered a direct hit in the bomb-bay which threw the B-17 into a spin. Only three crew escaped. It was back to Berlin on the 21st and three B-17s went down on this mis-

Incomplete Vee formation at top left indicates that yet another Ridgewell B-17 and its crew have moved into the MIA category. Some 131 aircraft suffered this fate during the Group's twenty-two months in combat.

sion. On target approach, fighters had knocked down LT Dassault flying 42-31980, flak then punched holes in twenty-seven of the remaining thirty-seven B-17s. LT Roy Pendergist (534th BS) was in *JOANNE* (4297174), the bomber which had been roasted during the 24 May mission, was set on fire by flak and Roy had barely followed his crew out when she exploded; sadly three SGTs were killed. LT Bailey (533th BS) was in *BABOON MCGOON* (42-38194) had already lost two engines from the fighter attacks and was forced to drop out. Unlike so many in this situation who were subsequently lost to either flak or fighters, the ailing B-17 was turned northwards for what turned out to be a successful attempt to cross the Baltic to Sweden. Meanwhile, on board the 535th BS Fortress, *BUTTON NOSE*, a cockpit fire caused LT Myerscough to be smothered in burning hydraulic fluid. SGT Rolla promptly smothered the flames with his hands then tackled the fire. The loss of hydraulics forced the pilots to use parachutes released from the rear to halt their bomber on landing and the same technique was used by LT J Winters in *MARSHA SUE*. Finally, to illustrate the extremes of fortune inherent in combat flying, LT Gilpin was struck in the chest by a flak fragment measuring 6 inches which knocked him out, but left him otherwise unharmed, the fifth time he had been hit in this region with his flak suit saving him each time.

Mission 141 on 22 June was significant, not as regards the target, but

This B-17 of the 534th Bomb Squadron was about to unload its bombs on the target area. The No 2 engine appears to have problems with oil spillage although the Wright Cyclone engine was inclined to throw oil. The aircraft was declared MIA with LT Rayburn on 19 April 1944 over Eschwege.

45

CENTURY NOTE (in the foreground) and another 532nd BS bomber ease their way past an uncomfortably close pattern of flak bursts. Both aircraft carry the "wedge-shaped" tail gun mounting which was replaced on later B-17Gs by the Cheyenne tail turret.

Although *MINNIE THE MERMAID* is camouflaged, her Division triangle on the wing is Black rather than White. The outer wing section was Natural Metal and the identification code letter spacing was unusual with the indivual aircraft letter at a higher level.

because it was the Group's first combat anniversary. Three twelve-strong formations went over in the face of light but accurate flak which set LT Peak's 42-97084 on fire. Then, a wing detached and eight of the crew went down in the spinning aircraft. Two days later and as the Group was bombing a bridge at Tours/La Roche, 42-102585 (LT Romasco) became yet another flak victim. The Radio/Operator Gunner was reported as blown out while, after a few minutes, the B-17 started a slow turn to the right and descended on fire with the tail section separating. Only Romasco and three other men came out intact.

June saw the Group achieve the highest monthly mission tally so far, twenty-three. One aspect of the increased pace in missions was the relative speed with which crewmen were completing them. For example,

SGT Warren Walker had commenced on 18 April and finished up on 15 June. As the Allied ground offensive was consolidated in readiness for the advance which was to ultimately sweep the Germans out of France and Belgium, the 8th was lending its support to the Army, as well as punching away at German industry. Ridgewell's thirty-six missions in July and August produced some twenty-four in the strategic category. By now the number of bombers despatched each time was nearly equivalent to what had comprised a CBW in 1943 terms.

Unknown to the 381st BG combat crews was the fact that aircraft loss-

A formation of 381st BG B-17Fs without the division triangle on the fin. The letter "L" on nearest B-17F is the individual aircraft letter, not a Group identification.

This unidentified B-17G displays severe battle damage to the tail. The tail gunner's fate was unknown but he would be fortunate to have escaped serious injury or even death.

es would never again approach the levels of first Schweinfurt or Oschersleben missions. Instead, there would be the occasional one or two bombers MIA, no consolation for the luckless crews, but a general relief for the remainder. The absence of fighters which had caused the most grief up to mid-1944 would be replaced by a more insidious menace — flak. As the 8th concentrated on key industries such as oil, these were quickly reinforced by 88MM and 120MM flak batteries. The most infamous at Merseberg/Leuna deployed some 500 weapons along the bombing approach. This form of assault would take a toll of bombers up to the end of the war.

Independence Day saw the first occasional loss when a variety of bridges were assigned. Bad weather forced a diversion to Tours/La Riche airfield. Some twenty minutes out LT Bobrof's *TOUCH THE BUTTON NELL II* lost an engine and dropped out. Bombs were jettisoned, but the No 3 engine failed as Bobrof tried to regain the formation and he turned for home under P-38 escort. Gear was thrown out, but as the descent reached 10,000 feet, the B-17 snapped into a spin from which only TGST Word and SGT Hitchcock escaped; one other man got out but cruelly snagged his harness on a stationary propeller blade and went in with the bomber. As Word floated down, he observed the pilots almost succeeding in correcting the spin and making a proper belly-landing but the angle of impact was still too steep to prevent disintegration and an explosion from which no survivors emerged.

The V-I Flying bomb Offensive was in full swing after nearly a month's operations and although the Allied medium bombers were taking on most of the attacks against the launch sites in the Pas de Calais there were calls for the heavies to add their weight whenever possible. Over 1,300 B-17s and B-24s went out on 6 July hitting V-sites with similar attacks two days later. Munich was an important industrial city as well as the emotional "heart" of the Nazi party. Its railroads and city center were the focus for three successive days efforts between 11 and

"Hogshead" shapes are 500 pound general purpose bombs being rolled into Ridgewell's bomb dump. The dump was primitive and consisted of protective earth mounds covered by camouflage netting.

13 July but bad weather on all three days forced the use of H2X radar for aiming.

Turning back from assembly on the 13th was LT Houston in 44-6148. Several attempts to locate a runway in the low cloud conditions prevailing at the time proved abortive and with two engines failing in succession, the B-17 was desperately eased into a field just south of the base. The bomber's momentum with a full bomb load was not exhausted before it encountered a local railroad cutting into which it slid. Even so it was several minutes before part of the bomb load exploded, but for no obvious reason only Houston and LT Scruggs managed to crawl out via their cockpit windows and the remaining seven crew members perished. Scruggs was horribly burned and also suffered a broken leg. He crawled to as far as the embankment edge, reaching it just as the explosion took place. Once again a crew had fallen in non-combat circumstances.

Deep penetration runs continued with Augsburg (on the 16th) and beginning on 18 July. with four successive thrusts to Peenemunde, Lechfeld, Dessau and Schweinfurt. The sole loss was LT O'Black in 42-102663 over Peenemunde.

LT William's crew stand in the burnt-out elevator of their B-17G *JOANNE* on 24 May 1944. All fabric on the control surfaces was burned off after the aircraft flew through the explosion caused by two other Group bombers colliding. Williams is at the extreme right while copilot Paul Lear stands on the left.

SGT Nick Rotz of the 535th BS displays the flak fragment which would certainly have killed him had he not worn a reinforced helmet liner on 22 May 1944. The helmet had holes in it for radio ear phones.

Although he survived, SGT Floyd Hanson (535th BS) being led to the ambulance on 21 May 1944, was unlucky. A flak fragment hit his side where the front and rear sections of flak suit left a gap. Hanson flew survived his full tour of combat duty.

The American 1st Army was now due to launch a break-out attack in the St. Lo region and the B-17s and B-24s were called on to weaken German resistance. On the 24th ground haze prevented most from bombing but for those who did there was a tragedy of accidental release over Allied lines which killed some U.S. soldiers. The next day almost 90% bombed but two separate short bombing incidents left over 100 dead including GEN McNair, This accident occurred despite use of ground smoke markers to avoid such errors. Two Merseburg missions and then Munich rounded off July. The 8th was truly living up to its

"Mighty" image in terms of numbers despatched with a mission average of 1,200 of which between 80% and 90% made bombing runs.

Once again a month's beginning proved unlucky for three crews. On 3 August LT Wilcock in 42-32049 turned back en route to Mulhausen but failed to regain Ridgewell and next day his body was washed ashore, no others were ever found. Two days later LT Melomo flying Deputy Lead in 42-97771 was brought down by flak over the coast on the way in and next day saw LT Webb's 44-6020 downed. Assembly on the 4th was marred when the Deputy Lead's 42-97594 caught fire and crashed near Wethersfield, but only the tail gunner failed to jump. On board as

Belting ammunition was a monotonous job, but care had to be taken to ensure the rounds were properly mounted to avoid jamming of the bomber's .50 caliber machine guns.

Bomb-bay tanks were sometimes carried, although the 2,840 gallion capacity main tanks permitted B-17Gs to reach most targets with fuel to spare. Bomb loads were reduced whenever the bomb bay tanks were fitted.

Century Note was well named because it survived that number of missions. Absence of 1st CBW color markings indicate that this was prior to July of 1944, when these markings were introduced.

A Varga girl adorns the nose of *SLEEPY TIME GAL* (42-107112), a 532nd BS B-17G which was the regular bomber flown by LT Dave Morgan's crew. Both the aircraft and its crew survived the war.

an observer was CAPT Francis Hawkins (Group Photographic Officer) - records do not state whether he flew further missions following his parachute descent.

The mix of strategic and tactical missions reflected the impending Allied ground offensive as well as the need to maintain pressure on German industry. Sometimes these over-lapped as when railroad stations and yards were hit at Saarbricken (9th) and Emden (27th). The aviation industry received attention with Brandenburg (6th), Halle (16th) and Neubrandenburg (25th) while Metz/Frescaty and Ostheim airfields were struck on consecutive days. The sheer pace of operations caused COL Leber to wistfully remark to CBW HQ that both crews and aircraft could do with a stand-down, especially the latter, since he was tired of "flying my wagons on three engines." Although much of the flak damage left little external evidence the fragments often played havoc with the internal framework and mechanics of the B-17s. Further large-scale Army support attacks were made on the 8th this time around Caen in the British sector upon which much of the German armor had been drawn. Bombing from a low 14,000 feet they met with heavy flak which fatally crippled the Deputy Lead carrying CAPT Tom Barnicle(42-37704). It was a full week before full details became available. A burst in the bomb-bay started a fire and further concussion tore the extinguisher from the hands of TSGT Glover as he fought the blaze. The flames spread to the right wing and LT Beackley called for bail-out. All per-

LT Art Bailey (standing, left) and his 532nd BS crew in front of FRENCHY'S FOLLY on 11 November 44. The officer in middle is holding the crew's mascot, a ferocious Manchester Terrier.

sonnel landed behind Canadian front-line positions and their B-17 smashed into a vacant schoolhouse. Barnicle's luck followed him to the C-47 base from which he and most of the crew flew back to Ridgewell because he played in a crap game and won a tidy pile of dollars.

COL Leber's keen desire for a stand-down was granted next day and the 448th Sub Depot engineers got down to work doubtless grumbling at being restricted to base until full flying status for all Fortresses was achieved. This was seemingly satisfied within forty-eight hours since the Group flew to bomb harbor installations at Brest on the 11th. Similar tactical operations to a Rouen-road junction led to mortal wounds for a 535th BS navigator LT Haines; flak severed one leg and virtually severed the other and poor Haines bled to death, becoming the first squadron fatality in many weeks. The penultimate August mission was briefed for Berlin, but bad weather forced a recall with targets of opportunity in Emden being bombed.

August witnessed a great contrast in Allied fortunes in Europe. At the start, German resistance was causing no deal of concern at Allied ability to break through at least around Caen. Without this movement there was little or no chance of beating the enemy by U.S. Army advances alone. However by mid-August both arms of the ground "pincer" were squeezing the German 7th Army in the Falaise region and although many troops did escape they left their equipment behind. The hunt was

Another beautiful Varga girl was painted on FORT WORTH GAL, a B-17 of the 533rd BS. The bomber failed to return from Gaggenau on 10 September 1944.

This B-17G (42-31570) was named *LUCKY ME* and served with the 533rd BS. The Fortress came to Ridgewell on 2 February 1944 and was ultimately declared Missing In Action on 25 September 1944 over Frankfurt.

on and while the U.S. forces drove towards Alsace/Lorraine the British/Canadian units thrust up into Northern France and through to Belgium. There seemed a real prospect that Germany could be entered and a total surrender brought about before 1944 ended if this rate of advance could be sustained.

A full-blooded return to strategic bombing was the order for September with one notable exception on the 17th when Operation MARKET GARDEN was set in motion. This was a daring attempt to seize bridges over the Dutch rivers, especially the Rhine bridge at Arnhem, to allow armored columns to sweep up the cleared corridor and round into the Ruhr. History records how the gallant failure to hold Arnhem basically doomed the plan to failure. But hopes were high on that bright Sunday morning as the C-47s, Stirlings and Halifaxes set out with gliders in tow. The 381st BG bombed gun locations around Eindhoven and GEN Brereton the CinC of the Airborne Forces flew in a 534th BS B-17 in order to observe the assembly of the C-47 formations.

Ludwigshafen's oil refineries became the repeated center of attention for attacks with four separate missions of which the 381st BG joined in

THE FOX was a 534th BS B-17G named after the local pub situated near the squadron dispersals. She lasted until 14 February 1945 when she was shot down during the Dresden mission.

two (3rd and 8th) and the continuing importance of oil was emphasized by two runs to Merseberg and one to Brux ,Czechoslovakia. Otherwise target selection mainly involved marshaling yards. Light flak was met over Gaggenau on the 10th which brought down LT Germano in *FORT WORTH GAL* (44-6095). The uncertain Autumn weather forced regular use of H2X and Group notes comment that Osnabruck (26th) was the first mission in seven days on which visual bombing runs were made. Frankfurt the day before recorded the sole other monthly loss in this case *LUCKY ME* (42-31570) but all crew including SGT Hal Mourning exited the burning B-17 after flak hit her on the bomb-run. Hal's precaution of tying his walking shoes to his harness proved of no avail as the opening shock caused the securing string to break.

The rumors of super-fast enemy aircraft gaining currency in USAAF ranks since mid-Summer were now being regularly confirmed. On 7 October, *LOS ANGELES CITY LIMITS* (42-107018) flown by LT O'Connor (both 535th BS) sustained flak strikes over the target which tore away much of the bomb-bay doors and disabled two engines. Straggling out of formation the B-17 soon attracted the attention of two or three ME-163s. Even in this extreme of peril, the pilots maneuvered their "cripple" sufficiently to avoid the several passes made, fortunately not together, by the German fighters and after five or ten minutes P-51s came on the scene to harry the enemy out of the area.

Schweinfurt held bad memories for those personnel still around from mid-1943 since it was the scene of the Group's worst defeat. Therefore when the curtains were pulled off the briefing-room board on 9 October the tension most have soared. Hardly the manner in which to celebrate the Group's 200th mission. The weather, however, proved to be the toughest obstacle with clouds forcing a PFF bomb-run while flak was meager and fighters were totally absent. Plans for a 200 mission party were turned down by GEN Williams following bad disturbances at similar Division events which reputedly involved one suicide and one murder.

Three runs to Cologne's railroad system began the third century of missions and for the rest of October targets all over Germany were attacked. A bonus to the well-worked crews was five days free of missions. Hamburg was Germany's second industrial city and was accordingly well defended by flak. The 381st BG led on 6 November but H2X was used as the clear weather faded away on the final approach The privilege of being Lead Group was soured by two losses. The 535th BS had flown sixty-four missions without loss but a flak burst on the bomb-run hit the No. 3 engine on *CHUGALUG IV* (42-97330) and she dropped out. LT Levitoff was flying wingman to the H2X aircraft and his action of salvoing the bombs caused the Group's rear elements to treat this as a release signal; being two minutes short of the IP, these loads missed the target area. LT Dudley Brommet's B-17 was hit and

Edward G. Robinson christens this overall Natural Metal B-17G named HAPPY BOTTOM on 5 July 1944 watched by COL Leber (right) and the 532th BS bomber's crew-chief, SGT Joe Hudrick, who was leaning out of the cockpit.

abandoned by all nine men, although LT Bill Barker received a bad ankle wound which earned him a post-war disability pension. The perils of close formation flying and of being "bombed" by surrounding B-17s was shockingly demonstrated over Cologne on 10 Nov. As LT Metts in *HELLS ANGEL* (42-97265) was nearing the release point, his bomber was struck by three 110 pound bombs. Two of these sheered off the nose but the third came into the area forward of the astrodome and hit LT Drummond on the head with fatal results. For the next forty-five minutes the surviving crew suffered the agony of being unable to free the bomb but finally it was dislodged and jettisoned via the nose hatch. The traumatic effect of losing a buddy was such that all personnel were hospitalized over-night.

As autumn turned into winter, the bright cries of "Home for Xmas" echoed around September were all but silenced. The war would clearly be prolonged until favorable weather conditions in Spring of 1945

allowed the Allies to cross the Rhine and gain decisive command of the German hinterland. The pace of bombing missions was also slowing down in the face of what would be one of the worst European winters for years. The second half of November involved the 381st BG in six of the seven missions despatched; oil was the primary target struck and this month would witness the culmination of regular attacks on this industrial resource. Bombing a general area with H2X methods was imprecise enough with an average circular error of two miles but when, on the 26th, it was used to hit a railroad bridge near Altenbecken, MAJ Bill Fullick (Group Bombardier) tersely reported at interrogation, "I think we hit a field."

Despite the fiercely defended nature of oil targets there were no aircraft losses but on the Zeitz mission (30th), the 532th BS had LT Guise abort and on landing leveled off too high over the runway threshold the resultant heavy impact on landing caused the right landing gear to collapse. The bomb load and fuel from ruptured tanks cascaded along the runway, although, miraculously the anticipated explosion never occurred.

December commenced with a milkrun to Soest followed next day by a 5/6 hour gunnery practice flight, very boring but questionably safer. Only four more missions were flown in the next ten days. On 16 December, the Germans launched an offensive under bad weather conditions that persisted for the next seven days. Once this cleared, an Anglo/American counterattack on both sides of the "Bulge" created by the enemy on rush drove the Germans back.

Heavy bomber operations in this frustrating week were limited and, in Ridgewell's case, restricted to one mission to bomb Cologne marshaling yards on 18 Dec. Otherwise, the fog had caused cancellations and the crews's sense of frustration was deepened by the reports from the Ardennes and the airmens' inability to intervene. Therefore the briefing on Christmas Eve was greeted with relative pleasure according to LT Kelley, a 535th BS navigator. COL Leber told the men that the weather was clearing over the Continent and a mission was going out despite the fog shrouding the English bases. In his words, "We are going to give our ground forces a Christmas present they will never forget." That

TOMAHAWK WARRIOR of the 535th Bomb Squadron is shrouded by a typical English fog during the Spring of 1945. She blew up after making an emergency landing, after returning from practice mission on fire.

The lead bomber turns onto the northeast end of the short runmay at Ridgewell. Narrow, fifty foot perimeter tracks did not permit much margin for erior when taxing what were unwieldy and often heavily-laden Fortresses.

days total of 2,046 heavies far exceeded the previous maximum of 1,586 despatched a week before. Some Groups even sent their Formation Assembly aircraft.

Airfields and communication centers in Western Germany were the selected targets and Ridgewell's fifty-one bombers were split between Ettinhausen and Kirchgons airfields. As LT Kelley's force was making its bomb-run he was horrified to sight a B-24 Group approaching head-on to the 381st BG with its High Squadron directly in line with his Low Squadron. Miraculously no collisions took place, but as the B-24s headed away one was observed to explode. Fog conditions were forming as the short winter day faded beneath the home-coming B-17s and B-24s and a number of airfields in the Midlands were already "socked in." The resultant diversion to Ridgewell of around seventy-five bombers from such bases would place some strain on 381st BG personnel, particularly the cooks.

Although Xmas Day saw no respite for the 8th, the persistent fog kept the 1st BD on the ground and two more days elapsed before it again undertook an operation. The railroad bridge chosen on the 28th for attack held no special significance, Remagen on the Rhine. The bridge remained unscathed from this and succeeding attacks. This was supremely ironic since it was across this very structure three months later that U.S. Army units rushed to secure a totally unexpected foothold in the German heartland. Missions to Mainz rail yards and a communications center at Prum rounded off the 381st BG's combat record for 1944.

British ATS servicewoman PVT Cynthia Burfield christens *SMASHING TIME* on 2 September 1944; this was her prize for winning a beauty contest the previous evening. The overall Natural Metal B-17G (43-38158) belonged to the 534th BS.

1945

As 1945 began, the 8th's bombing campaign had but 125 days to run. By now the bombers were ranging almost at will over Central Europe but the enemy was still exacting what was admittedly a steadily diminishing price in destroyed B-17s and B-24s along with their crews. In this remaining period of combat, the 381st BG would fly sixty-eight missions, one every two days.

The newly titled 1st Air Division hit a variety of targets on 1 January but the 381st BG seems to have been the sole unit to hit its assigned target, although with but eleven of the thirty-seven bombers despatched. While proceeding out over the North Sea and flying in between two layers of solid clouds, the Group Leader elected to climb the formation. The inevitable occurred with the B-17s emerging in a well scattered pattern. By the time reassembly was effected, the Group had lost its place in the Divisional formation. Bad weather over Merseberg forced two "dummy" bomb-runs and as the third was completed, 42-37553 lost power on both starboard-side engines. LTs Peters and Nelson fought to keep their B-17 airborne but since both functioning engines were forcing the Fortress into a potential spin when level flight was attempted they had no alternative but to accelerate into a shallow but steady dive. A course for an emergency airfield near Brussels, Belgium was set but it was fifty anxious minutes before Allied lines were re-crossed near Metz. By then the ailing bomber was at 1,500 feet and clearly would never make Brussels. LT Kelley was among the last to abandon the aircraft via the bomb-bay and despite a double somersault on landing only sprained a thumb. Two approaching GIs ordered him to put up his hands; they had been alerted to a possible parachute attack following up

A pair of B-17Gs of the 533rd BS with *DREAMBABY* in the fore-ground. *DREAM BABY* survived the war, but *LUCKY* ME (back-ground) was Missing In Action on 25 September 1044.

Another 532nd BS B-17G was *UNDER GROUND FARMER*, English name slang for a miner. She carried a partial female figure on the nose and had the serial 44-6020. The Fortress was declared MIA on 6 August 1944.

on operation BODENPLATTE, the mass Luftwaffe fighter assault on Allied continental airfields carried out this very day. Kelley pointed to his B-17 fast disappearing out of sight and this indicator coupled with his very American accent convinced the GIs he was friendly. Taken to a Military Police station, Kelley was there re-united with three other crewmen. Eventually, all nine men were accounted for. SGT Giannacopoulis broke a leg and was then shipped back to the States. SGT Bolin was rescued from a minefield while SGT Knaus survived being shot at by a group of GIs in a truck as he floated down. Four of this crew were to feature in another B-17s loss in late March which had

Pair of "Mickey" ships lead a Group formation on the bomb-run during mid-1944. "Mickey" B-17s had radar pods replacing their the ball turets. The lower aircraft belongs to either the 303rd BG or 384th BG.

a more tragic outcome.

Returning crews were more weary than usual because of an official "mis-understanding." The previous evening at the regular Group party session they had been assured by a Brigadier General that they were officially "stood down" and had over-celebrated. Most of the men called for the mission were still drunk and probably only a mixture of coffee and pure oxygen enabled them to function properly. Only five made it back to Ridgewell with the remainder scattered around France, Belgium and England. Kelley's crew took eight days to get back via Nancy ,France and Brighton with the final stage being accomplished by railroad.

The fourteen missions flown in January started off with continuing

This B-17G of the 535th BS was named *LOS ANGELES CITY LIMITS*. She was on final approach and had just flared out as her pilots eased her over the runway threshold at Ridgewell during the Summer of 1944.

emphasis on shattering the enemy ground offensive. Aiming points were sometimes limited to map co-ordinates as on the 3rd, but on this occasion the Group diverted to its secondary at Cologne; even then PFF bombing methods were compulsory due to 10/10 cloud. The weatherman seemed to be on Hitler's side according to the 535th BS diarist when "a nice fat cloud" over Heimbach's rail yard completely negated the otherwise clear sky condition on the bomb-run. On this occasion, the Radio Beam System known as G-H was used as on the next day's mission to the same target and this was becoming a regular feature of assisted bombing whenever cloud intervened. Attempting to hit narrow outline targets such as the Rhine bridge at Germersheim on the 13th with such a method was very optimistic and although some crews said one end was bracketed no definite damage was confirmed.

Although oil facilities were back on the priority list from the 14th, the 1st AD was largely being allocated bridges and railroad yards during the month with the other two ADs taking on the former task. COL Leber flew the last of his thirty missions on the 21st but any sense of celebra-

The badly damaged bomb-bay on LOS ANGELES CITY LIMITS is examined by her officer complement following the 7 October 1944 mission when the aircraft and crew survived attacks by three Me 163 rocket-propelled fighters. The damage to the bomb bay was was caused by flak.